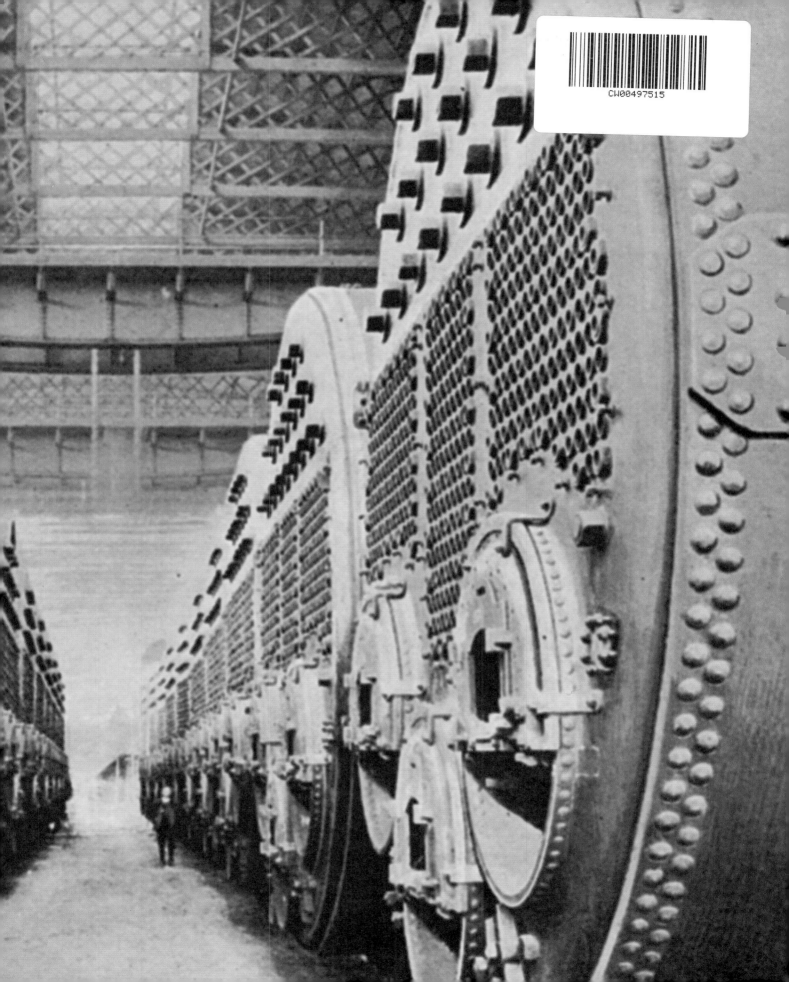

TITANIC

~ 1912 ~

igloobooks

igloobooks

Published in 2015
by Igloo Books Ltd
Cottage Farm
Sywell
NN6 0BJ
www.igloobooks.com

SHE001 0715
2 4 6 8 10 9 7 5 3 1
ISBN 978-1-78440-209-9

Written by Kim Aitken

Front cover image © Popperfoto / Getty Images
Back cover image © Thinkstock / Getty Images

Printed and manufactured in China

TITANIC
～❧ 1912 ❧～

Contents

THE TITANIC

Introduction

The largest cruise ship in the world at the time, the Titanic fatefully sank to the bottom of the ocean on its maiden voyage in 1912 from Southampton, England to New York City, United States of America. Now arguably the most famous ship in history, fascination with how *'the unsinkable ship'* could have encountered such a cruel end continues today.

The Titanic's infamy came from its collision with an iceberg crossing the North Atlantic, after which the ship sank quickly. The resulting deaths of over 1500 people made it one of the most ill-fated ocean disasters ever. Until it sank, it was the largest ship on the water in the world. Although uniquely well known by today's young and old alike, the ship itself was not unique. It was one of three enormous liners built in Belfast, Ireland.

Royal Mail Steamer (RMS) Titanic carried some of the wealthiest passengers in the world. Designed and marketed to attract a clientele who sought luxury and first-class travel, Titanic was an exciting new maritime and travel development.

With opulent accommodation, classy restaurants, swimming pool and gymnasium, it was the most exciting, sophisticated way to travel at the time. The liner offered glamour and adventure, a heady combination that garnered a lot of interest from the press and the public on its launch.

In addition to first-class passengers, the Titanic also offered an escape for the less fortunate and carried hundreds of passengers who were emigrating from Europe to America.

The captain of the Titanic, Edward J Smith, had sailed the route often and was aware of the iceberg dangers coming from the North Atlantic Ocean. Despite warnings, the ship avoided a head-on collision but was badly damaged after scraping along the side of an immense iceberg. The resulting rescue was a disaster, with only 705 people saved from some 2,200 passengers. Shocking the world with its fatalities, controversy and outrage followed for the builders, owners and leaders whose responsibility was the safety of passengers.

Above; Lifeboats on board the SS Titanic.

*Above; 10th April 1912. This illustration shows the White Star liner
Titanic leaving Southampton bound for New York.*

Main; The Titanic is being manoeuvred away from Berth 44 in Belfast wharf to begin her maiden voyage, 10th April 1912.

For many years, it was believed that the ship sank quickly because of a huge tear in the hull, but investigations later revealed the icy water had compromised the steel frame, causing it to fracture. The ship sank in less than three hours following the collision, breaking into two. There have been many reports on the building and materials used to make this ship and how they contributed to the sinking, although some of the findings remain unsubstantiated.

There are also many myths and mysteries surrounding the Titanic, causing it to continue to be a source of fascination for the media and public around the world. Its legacy lives on, with numerous investigations and inquests that follow today. Experts are still attempting to further understand what happened the day the Titanic sank, 15th April 1912. People continue to visit exhibitions and displays, watch television documentaries and movies made about this real life tragedy.

Over 100 years on, the Titanic's story has people enthralled with its journey and tragic ending.

Above; Café Parisien on board RMS Titanic, an extension to the First Class restaurant.

CONCEPT AND CONSTRUCTION

Owners & Builders

The detail behind construction of the world's most infamous ship offers greater understanding of the fateful end to its maiden voyage.

A competitive venture, the design and construction of the Titanic was the brainchild of J. Bruce Ismay, chairman of White Star Line. Ismay teamed up with shipbuilders Harland and Wolff, a shipbuilder company originally formed in 1861. Established by Edward James Harland and Hamburg-born Gustav Wilhelm Wolff, the company began its business by purchasing a small shipyard on Queen's Island, Belfast, Ireland.

Earning a reputation for developing innovative ships with iron upper decks instead of wood, they were credited with strengthening ships at the time. Following Harland's death in 1895, Lord William James Pirrie was appointed chairman and Thomas Andrews the general manager and head of the draughting in 1907.

On their appointment to build the Titanic, the company was looking to further innovate the shipbuilding industry.

Above: Bruce Ismay,
Chairman of the White Star Line.

Main; Captain John Smith (1850 - 1912) and Lord James Pirrie, Chairman of the Harland & Wolff Shipyard, on the deck of the White Star Liner.

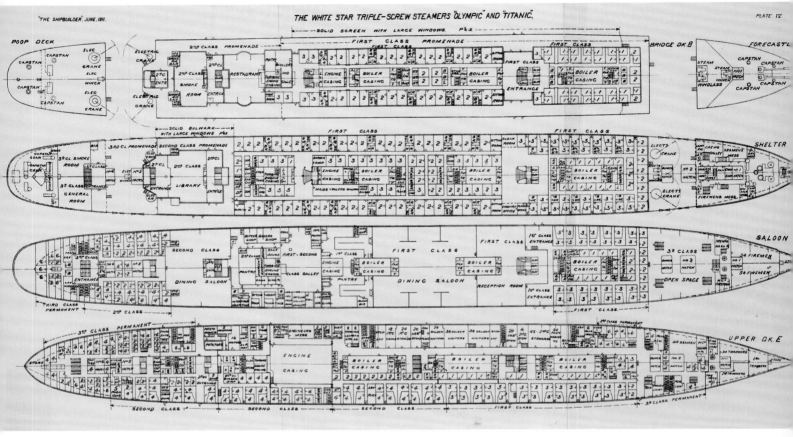

Above; Plans of the liners built by Harland & Wolff in Belfast.

It was predicted that the Titanic, along with its sisters the Gigantic and Olympic, was to be roughly one and a half times the size of their competitor's (Cunard Line) ships.

Following a long relationship history with the White Star Line (dating back to 1867), the builders were offered what was considered to be a lot of freedom to design and construct the trio of Olympic ships. The building company was apparently also given authorization to invest financially in what they needed to create the liners, as well as a 5 percent margin to retain on the final cost.

Above; Mr Andrews,
Managing Director of Harland and Wolff.

Harland and Wolff's top designers were engaged to plan and draw concepts for the innovative liners overseen by Lord Pirrie, who was both a director of the builders and of the White Star Line. Thomas Andrews, who died in the disaster that followed, was a naval architect and managing director of the design department. Lord Pirrie's nephew, Thomas Andrews was at the height of his career. He prepared the scale drawings that would enable work to start. Andrews' second-in-charge was Edward Wiling, who was responsible for calculating the stability and trim of the design. Finally, Harland and Wolff's Alexander Carlisle was the man responsible for equipment, decorations and lifeboat design.

Right; The White Star Line vessels Olympic and Titanic under construction in Harland and Wolff's shipyard, Belfast, Northern Ireland, 1909-1911.

On the 1st July, 1907 the builders were instructed to begin work in preparation for the construction of the two ships.

The Titanic was allocated the shipyard number 401 and the Olympic 400.

In July of 1908, one short month later, the design drawings were approved by the White Star Line and construction commenced. Just over 269 metres (882 feet 9 inches) long, the Titanic's design was ambitious. It was dangerous to build such a vast ship. Indeed, no ship building company had embarked on a construction of this size and nature before; the ship's breadth was an incredible 28.19 metres (92 feet 6 inches) and height was 32 metres (104 feet).

The sheer size of the three ships meant a new approach was required. In Belfast Harbour, on Queen's Island, Harland and Wolff demolished three slipways to make room for two new slipways, the largest ever made at the time. This is now known as the Titanic Quarter.

Building began in March 1909, after alterations were made to the shipyard to accommodate the sheer size of the liners. The White Star Dock and the Great Gantry were constructed specially and provided huge cranes, which were able to lift up to 200 tons. These cranes would carry materials and men to the height of the deck, nearly 150 feet up.

Fig. 25.—Tank Top and After End Framing of the "Olympic." (30th July, 1909.)

Above; Tank top and after end framing of the Olympic, 13th July 1909.

Left; The stern of the Cunard liner Olympic at the Harland and Wolff yard, Belfast, just prior to her launch. Known as 'Old Reliable', she was the sister ship of the Titanic and Britannic.

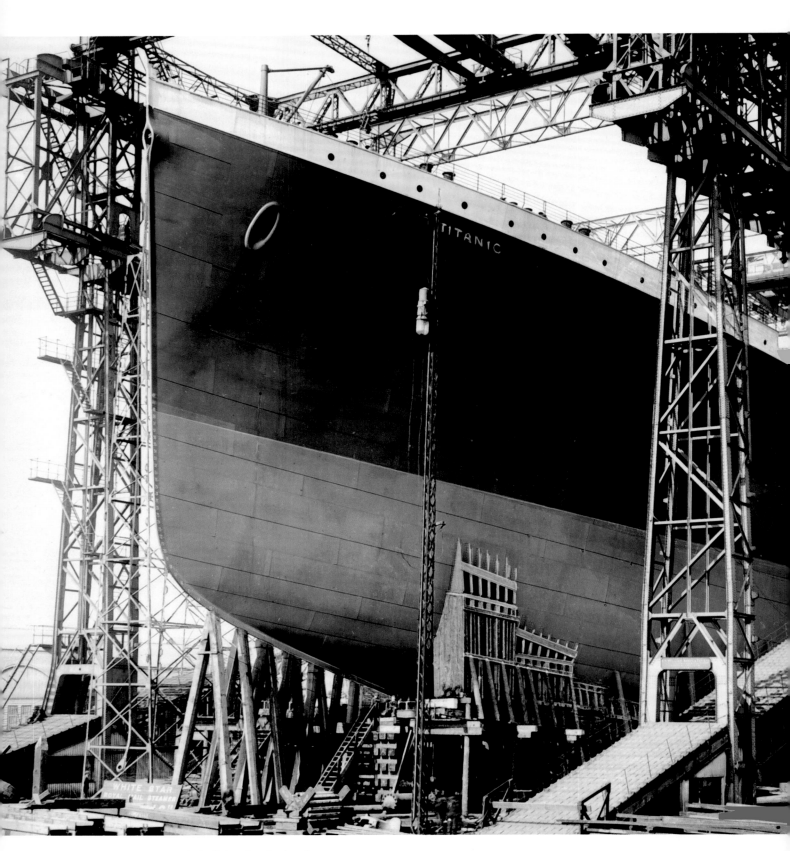

*Main; : The Titanic photographed at the Harland and Wolff shipyard in Belfast during the
Spring of 1911. The ship was launched on 31st May 1911 and then spent a further year
being fitted out prior to its disastrous maiden voyage in April 1912.*

ir William Arrol & Co, a Scottish company, which had previously built London's Tower Bridge, was employed to build The Arrol or Great Gantry, which stood 69 metres (228 feet) high, 260 metres long (840 feet) and 82 metres (270 feet) wide. It weighed 6000 tons and was, fittingly, the largest gantry in the world at the time.

Large enough to accommodate at least 10 mobile cranes that were used to transport men and materials, The Great Gantry was capable of supporting a huge amount of space and machinery. A floating crane that was engineered to lift 200 tons was also imported from Germany.

Above; A stern view of the White Star Liner, RMS Titanic, docked at Queenstown (Cobh) on 11th April 1912.

Above; A photograph of passengers on the promenade deck, showing the lifeboats to the left.

The Titanic and Olympic would be built in parallel, side-by-side using the same construction process. Each taking 26 months to build, the Olympic's hull was completed first (in December 1908) and the Titanic's in March of 1909.

The keel acted as a backbone and the frame of the hull formed the *'ribs'* of the ship. The frames were then covered in an enormous skin of steel.

Incredibly, the steel skin consisted of 2,000 pieces of steel, which was delivered in rolls. Each plate was between 2.5cm (1 inch) to 3.8cm (1.5 inches) thick and was up to 9.1 metres (30 feet) long. The plates were laid across from the keel to the bilge by overlapping the edges. From here, they were laid one plate in and one plate out (or over), to the top of the frame.

As the technique of welding was still new, the steel structure had to be held together with over three million iron and steel rivets. On their own, these weighed more than 1200 tons.

It would take three years in total to build and fit out the Titanic. By April of 1908, the frame of the ship was already complete.

Construction was then organised around the requirements for eight main decks. To build it safely, innovative techniques and modern materials had to be used. Building the liners also required the hard graft and labour of thousands of men, some of whom who lost their lives during the construction. It was reported that 17 men lost their lives building the Titanic and the Olympic. Sadly, this included a father and son.

According to reports, eight of those men lost their lives while building the Titanic. This was considered to be fewer than expected for the size of the project. One report describes an expectation of loss of up to 15 lives for a build of this size and nature. In total, there were 15,000 men who worked for the company at the time and the work was carried out without protective hats or hand guards while operating machinery. Such exposed, dangerous work meant that during the construction of the Titanic, there were 246 injuries recorded, 28 of which were termed 'severe'. This meant many men lost limbs while attempting to build, crushed under the weight of heavy steel.

Main; The massive anchor of the White Star liner Titanic is transported to its destination in Belfast by horse-drawn cart.

The methods and materials employed for its construction were of the highest standard of its time, using newly discovered welding and imported steel. The steel was incorporated in the frame of the hull, cut and welded into huge plates, which were then painstakingly riveted on. Many labourers later complained of hearing difficulty from the noise of this riveting process. A four-man crew would complete roughly 200 rivets a day during the construction. Based on this, it would have taken 15,000 days of riveting for each four-man crew to complete the work.

Recent research, challenged by the builders Harland and Wolff, suggest poor quality iron was used to make three million rivets holding the hull plates together, which reportedly popped prematurely on collision with the fatal iceberg in 1912.

Along with many theories and myths regarding the sinking of the Titanic, there were unsubstantiated arguments that the ship sank quickly, because of the sealed, 'watertight compartments'. Considered a fantastic safety mechanism on build and launch, these 'watertight' rooms would later come under scrutiny for their role in the sinking of the mighty vessel. However, subsequent reports have indicated it is unlikely the watertight compartments accelerated the sinking.

"Let the Truth be known, no ship is unsinkable. The bigger the ship, the easier it is to sink her. I learned long ago that if you design how a ship'll sink, you can keep her afloat. I proposed all the watertight compartments and the double hull to slow these ships from sinking. In that way, you get everyone off. There's time for help to arrive and the ship's less likely to break apart and kill someone while she's going down."

Thomas Andrews, Managing Director of Harland and Wolff Shipyards

With ten decks in total, eight of which would be for passenger use, the interior of each ship was divided into sixteen compartments. In the event of an emergency, there were 11 watertight doors installed, which were intended to seal off each compartment.

Up on deck, the flooring was made of pine and teak. Each of the two decks were roughly 150 metres (500 feet) long. They were named the Promenade Deck and Boat Deck and hosted officers' quarters, a gymnasium, public rooms and first-class cabins, as well as a bridge and wheelhouse.

Main; Titanic under construction in Belfast.

Above; A crew member and passengers on 'A' Deck, just under the bridge of the White Star liner Titanic, 11th April 1912.

"Control your Irish passions, Thomas. Your uncle here tells me you proposed 64 lifeboats and he had to pull your arm to get you down to 32. Now, I will remind you just as I reminded him these are my ships. And, according to our contract, I have final say on the design. I'll not have so many little boats, as you call them, cluttering up my decks and putting fear into my passengers."

J. Bruce Ismay, Director of the White Star Line

Lifeboats were then added to the Boat Deck, the upper deck. While the Titanic was designed to house more lifeboats than required by the maritime safety regulations as determined by the Board of Trade, this included only 20 lifeboats, 16 of which were made of wood and four that were collapsible. Too few for the number of crew and passengers on board, this would become a problem when the vessel collided on its voyage.

According to reports, Harland and Wolff's managing director Andrews wanted to include 64 lifeboats, but it was considered unsightly and would spoil the view for first-class passengers. There were other reports that passengers expected fewer lifeboats so they could enjoy the open space. As the size of ships had grown so quickly in such a short time – apparently up to 400 percent in 12 years – it would be difficult to foresee a disaster like that of the Titanic's to follow.

Four enormous funnels were installed, of which only three were actually functional and for use; the fourth was for aesthetic purposes, likely included to balance the look with four symmetrical funnels. Two masts were constructed and supported loading of cargo. A wireless telegraph aerial was also used, hung between the masts and 15 metres (50 feet) above the ship's funnels. This powerful aerial was provided for the convenience of passengers and for operational use.

The two 1.5kW spark-gap wireless telegraphs were installed in the radio room on the Boat Deck. One was used for transmitting messages and the other for receiving them. The system, owned and operated by the Marconi Company, was one of the most powerful in the world, apparently reaching a range of up to 1,000 miles.

While the Titanic was almost identical to sister ship Olympic, there were some changes introduced to set them apart from one another. The Titanic's Promenade Deck had a steel screen fitted, with sliding doors, to provide extra shelter to the first class passengers on board. This was added at the request of Bruce Ismay. Taking much longer to construct than expected, it was reported that the changes instructed by Ismay and some repairs required on the Olympic slowed its launch. The repairs made on the Olympic were ironically due to a collision the ship had in September 1911 after it launched.

Above; The Titanic is launched at the Harland and Wolff shipyard in Belfast, 31st May 1911.

The Titanic being heavier than the Olympic meant it was the largest ship in the world at the time. It weighed 46,328 gross register tons.

Launched on 31st May 1911, the Titanic was not given an official naming ceremony or christening with champagne. This was in line with the White Star Line's policy for all its ships. As well as Lord Pirrie, Morgan and Ismay and the Lord Lieutenant of Ireland, over 100,000 people watched the ship's passage into the River Lagan and witnessed the launch. It required 22 tons of soap and tallow to lubricate its entry into the water, which took only 62 seconds.

Following the launch, the ship was then towed to a fit-out berth, for the engines, funnels and interior to be installed.

The interior fit-out of the ship was opulent and impressive. Its crowning glory, the Titanic's Grand Staircase, was made from polished oak and wrought iron. The staircase was installed under a huge glass dome and descended seven decks, leading to ornate entrance halls lit by gold-plated lamps. The feature ornament of the Grand Staircase was a large carved wooden clock. A novelty for its time, the ship also featured elevators. Inside, the ceilings were painted with granulated cork in order to stave off condensation.

The ship being such a vast size, gave plenty of opportunity to extend its passengers in first class every luxury and convenience. Such grand interiors and facilities were considered the finest in design and craftsmanship, even by today's standards.

On the Boat Deck, first-class passengers could use a gymnasium, which featured state-of-the-art equipment including rowing machines and a mechanical horse.

There was also a Promenade Deck that was 166 metres (546 feet) long, reserved for first-class passengers and cabins, as well as a first-class lounge to socialise in and reading and writing rooms. With oak-panelled walls and decorations modelled on the Palace of Versailles, the lounge's craftsmanship was considered superb, especially the detailed elaborate wooden carvings. The reading and writing rooms were elegant, with white walls, a fire and bow windows enabling a view out to the deck.

Above; : Marconi Operators; Jack Phillips and friend. Jack lost his life when the steamship sank, he stayed at his post sending out SOS messages up to the last moment.

There were also public rooms for first-class passengers in the form of a smoking room (which was created in Georgian style with mahogany panels featuring mother of pearl), reception room, dining saloon and cafes. The reception room led to the dining room, which spanned the full width of the ship and seated 532 passengers. The room's decoration was carefully researched on the finest homes in England and featured oak furniture. Offering a fine dining experience, it had floor to ceiling French walnut panels, with mounted ornaments and lamps. The large bay windows were decorated with silk curtains.

"It was the last word in luxury. The tables were gay with pink roses and white daisies […] the stringed orchestra playing music from Puccini and Tchaikovsky. The food was superb: caviar, lobster, quail from Egypt, plovers' eggs and hothouse grapes and fresh peaches".

Mrs Walter Douglas, a first-class passenger who survived the shipwreck

Above; The First Class Lounge.

Main; First Class Staircase, sister ship Olympic.

The Promenade Deck was also home to the Verandah Café and Palm Courts, which featured chequered floors, wicker furniture and plants. On the middle deck, there was a swimming pool and Turkish baths. The Turkish baths were for first-class men only and required a $1 (4 shillings) fee. A new luxury on board a ship, they featured a steam room, a shampooing room and marble drinking fountain.

First-class cabins featured private toilet facilities, two bedrooms, two wardrobe rooms and a bathroom. There were 39 suites in total, as well as 350 less expensive standard first-class cabins featuring single beds.

Main; Titanic; 'A' Deck. (Promenade deck). Titanic, having left
Southampton on her maiden voyage is passing the Portuguese R.M.S.P
Tagus, 10th April 1912. The figure may be that of Captain Smith.

Below; Mail-bags and Trunks being loaded.

Right; RMS Titanic, White Star
Line's Olympic-class in Harland and
Wolff's shipyard, Belfast, Ireland.

Second-class passenger accommodation was also elegant. Passengers could enjoy public rooms decorated in oak panelled rooms modelled Louis XVI style. There was a library installed for second-class women to read and write, with mahogany furniture and a large bookcase. Second-class passengers could also enjoy dining in an oak panelled dining room capable of seating 2394 people.

Second class accommodation was available in two versions – cabins fitted with two or four rooms. The berths, or beds, were built into the walls of the cabins and were fitted with curtains for privacy. The cabins had a washbasin and shared bathrooms.

The lower deck contained a squash court and post office, as well as open space for third-class passengers. As the Titanic was designated a Royal Mail Ship, she needed room for mail and cargo also. There was 760 cubic metres (26,800 cubic feet) of space in the ship's holds allocated for the letters, parcels and valuables.

The upper deck contained further passenger accommodation. The Orlop Decks and the Tank Top were at the lowest level of the ship, below the waterline.

Third-class passengers also had a Smoke and General Room, although the General Room was panelled in less expensive pine and finished in enamel white with teak furniture. However less expensive, the builders had considered the comfort of the passengers and fitted out the Smoke Room with oak panels and teak furniture, as well as a comfortable Third Class Dining Room which could seat 470 passengers.

Accommodation rooms for third-class consisted of two to six berth rooms. There were only two bathtubs for more than 700 passengers in third-class.

The fit-out of the interior of the Titanic also required crew accommodation, which was designed and planned so that the crew and passengers would not mix.

The engine room staff accommodation was on the starboard side on the Lower, Middle, Upper and Saloon Decks, with spiral staircases connecting their rooms to the boiler and engine rooms.

The ship was fitted with three main engines, two reciprocating four-cylinder, triple-expansion steam engines and one centrally placed low-pressure Parsons turbine. Having used this same engine combination on another liner successfully, they enabled an efficient use of fuel and steam power.

The two reciprocating engines installed were enormous, being 19 metres (63 feet) long and 720 tons in weight. Powered by steam boilers, there were 29 installed, each weighing 91.5 tons. Requiring 176 firemen to service them, the furnaces used 600 tons of coal every day. This meant the men had to shovel 100 tons of ash off the ship into the ocean daily. The work was extremely difficult.

Each engine drove propellers, which were fitted in February of 1912. There were three propellers for each engine, the largest having a diameter of 7.2 metres (23.5 feet).

The builders also fitted the Titanic with a rudder so large that it required steering engines to move it.

The ship was equipped with waterworks that were capable of heating and pumping water to all parts of the liner, through a series of pipes and valves.

Following a final coat of paint and last additions, testing and trials for the Titanic commenced on 2nd April 1912. Minor adjustments and supervision of testing meant the ship could reach up to 21 knots in the right conditions. Steam generated from 29 boilers supported the engines, to create 15,000 horsepower. The Titanic also tested well to an emergency stop.

After a difficult schedule and even more challenging and for some fatal, work constructing the ship, the Titanic was ready for its first voyage. The design of the Titanic was considered such that it could withstand a collision and sail to safety for repair.

At a final cost of $7.5 million, the Titanic was ready. By today's standards, it would cost approximately $400 million (£260 million) to build and fit out.

Above; : One of the engines for the Titanic nearing completion in the Engine Works at the Harland and Wolff shipyard in Belfast, May 1911. Once constructed the engine was then dismantled and taken to the fitting-out wharf to be re-built in the Titanic's engine room.

Above; RMS Titanic 1911.

THE WORLD'S LARGEST CRUISE LINER

The Unsinkable Ship

It seems unbelievable people would be convinced that almost 50,000 tons of steel forming the world's largest cruise liner could not sink. Now that the Titanic sits approximately 2.5 miles (12,460 feet) down at the bottom of the Atlantic Ocean, it has been deemed ridiculous that the public and media believed and perpetuated the myth that it was unsinkable on its launch in 1912.

Even today, the shipbuilders Harland and Wolff deny the Titanic was advertised as 'unsinkable'. The builders suggest the term or use of the word *'unsinkable'* came from articles published in the Irish News and the Shipbuilder magazine. The word was not actually printed or used in promotions; in fact it is difficult to ascertain where the term began being used. It seems the myth came from a number of sources.

The Irish News and Belfast Morning News had reported on the construction of the hull of the Titanic, detailing an analytical review of the system of watertight compartments and electronic watertight doors. Their concluding statements described the vessel as practically unsinkable.

"God himself could not sink this ship!"

Unnamed Titanic crew member to embarking passenger,
Mrs Sylvia Caldwell

*Main; February 1912. The Titanic at
Harland and Wolff's shipyard.*

In addition, Shipbuilder magazine ran an article in 1911 on the construction of the liner and made the same conclusion.

The assumption that a ship could be unsinkable is indeed surprising. However, this assumption grew from the certainty and reassurance brought by watertight compartments and doors as reported in the media. Harland and Wolff were safety conscious and in addition to arguing the case for more lifeboats, they had proposed a subdivided passenger compartment system that could isolate a section of the ship from water should there be an emergency.

The compartments were deemed 'watertight' although they would never be truly so. Labelled in alphabetical order from A to P, there were 16 compartments with activated doors.

"The captain can, by simply moving an electric switch, instantly close the doors throughout, practically making the vessel unsinkable."

**Irish News and Belfast Morning News,
1st June 1911**

Above; Passengers strolling past the lifeboats.

Main; RMS Titanic During Fitting Out

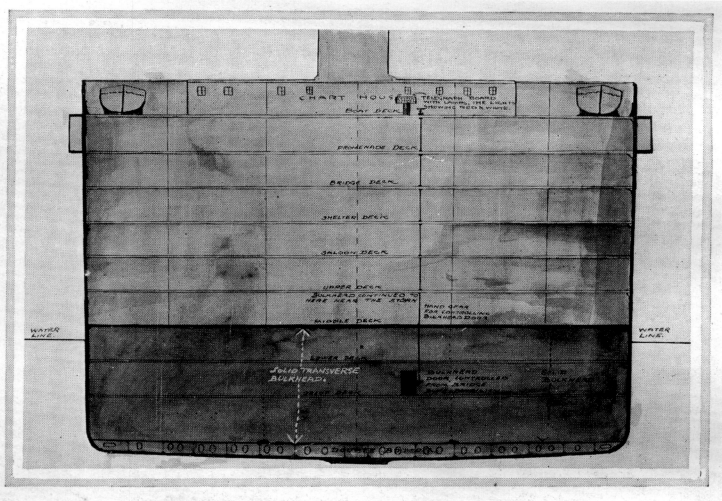

Bulkhead Arrangements on the "Titanic"

Main; Illustration showing a cross section of the bulkhead arrangements on Titanic.

To be absolutely watertight, the compartments would have needed to be enclosed within the hull, without passenger access between the rooms or through the halls. For a passenger cruise liner, this was not deemed practical or convenient. To accommodate this access, on the higher levels of passenger accommodation there were doors installed into the bulkheads, which meant it was impossible to keep any flooded compartment safe from flooding the remainder of rooms.

Above; 1894 rules required the largest category of vessels, those of '10,000 tons and upwards' to carry 16 lifeboats.

The practicality of this meant, again, the ship's legendary status as unsinkable was not feasible. However, there was some degree of reassurance provided by the fit-outs in the lower level compartments – those below waterline – where watertight doors were installed. These were Harland and Wolff's own design, hydraulically operated doors that would be operated by the captain and crew if necessary. With vertical sliding mechanism, they were considered state-of-the-art.

The doors had a friction clutch, which held the doors open. The control panel located on the bridge could release this clutch. Once activated, the doors could not be opened again. Only by remote control, from the switch on the panel, could they

be re-opened. There was also a float fitted to the door that would automatically close the door should it sense water at a dangerous level. On either of these activations, alarm bells would be triggered to warn crew members in the area in order to evacuate to the decks via emergency ladders.

In addition to safety fittings and the elusive guarantee of inclusions for an unsinkable ship, the Titanic was fitted with all available luxuries and modern comforts at the time. The Titanic's design and fit-out was incredibly safe and comfortable, as it was designed not for speed or risk but with the passengers in mind. However, the owner's consideration of passenger safety did not necessarily include passenger rescue.

Main; Extra lifeboats after the Titanic disaster. Berthon collapsible lifeboats fitted on RMS Majestic in addition to the normal rigid lifeboats.

The Boat Deck, on which the lifeboats were positioned, was segmented into separate promenades for officers, first-class, engineers and second-class passengers. The lifeboats lined the side of the deck, with the exception of the first class section so as not to spoil the view. The compromise of safety for aesthetics would be considered unwise after the Titanic's disaster.

It was on this deck that lifeboats would end up being lowered into the water in the early hours of 15th April 1912. There were only enough lifeboats for just under 1,200 people, which was only slightly more than half the number of passengers travelling on that maiden voyage. Including the crew, it was a mere one-third of the number required. Each lifeboat had the capacity to rescue 65 people each and the collapsible boats a capacity of only 47 people each. Stowed securely on the deck, they had been tested and lowered before the voyage.

Main; The largest vessel afloat at the time.

The decision to limit the number of lifeboats for aesthetic reasons was backed up by the belief that the ship was *'unsinkable'* and that if there were a collision or emergency, the design of the liner allowed her to remain afloat for a rescue and transport to repair. The inclusion of lifeboats was never considered in the context of the possibility that the ship could sink.

Because of this assumption that the Titanic was unsinkable, the crew was inadequately trained to use and manage the lifeboats, which meant that on rescue many of the lifeboats were half-empty and the evacuation itself was painfully slow.

Harland and Wolff built the lifeboats in the same location as the ship herself. Designed to avoid flooding by waves, they were given a double-end or two bows. They also added airtight copper tanks inside to give the boats extra buoyancy.

A promotional brochure published by the White Star Line in 1910, designed to advertise the Olympic and Titanic ships, made the suggestion by stating that they were designed to be unsinkable. The brochure, however, does not explicitly state that they were made to be or claimed to be unsinkable.

The White Star Line's Vice-President, Phillip Franklin, was more outspoken however. He would later come to regret the statement that it would not sink.

"There is no danger that Titanic will sink. The boat is unsinkable and nothing but inconvenience will be suffered by the passengers."

Phillip Franklin, White Star Line Vice-President

"The fact that Titanic carried boats for little more than half the people on board was not a deliberate oversight, but was in accordance with a deliberate policy that, when the subdivision of a vessel into watertight compartments exceeds what is considered necessary to ensure that she shall remain afloat after the worst conceivable accident, the need for lifeboats practically ceases to exist and consequently a large number may be dispensed with."

Archibald Campbell Holms in an article for Practical Shipbuilding, 1918

Some have suggested enthusiastic members of the White Star Line further perpetuated the myth that the Titanic was unsinkable.

"The press is calling these ships unsinkable and Ismay's leading' the chorus. It's just not true."

Thomas Andrews, Managing Director of Harland and Wolff Shipyards

Above; Survivors of the Titanic disaster board a GWR (Great Western Railway) ferry at Plymouth after arriving in England on the SS Lapland.

Main; Thomas Henry Ismay, founder of the White Star Line, late 19th century.

WHITE STAR LINE

The Quest for Grandeur

Founded in Liverpool in 1845, by John Pilkington and Henry Wilson, the White Star Line began its shipping fortune leasing and chartering ships to service the Australian gold mine trade. Instead of purchasing vessels, Pilkington and Wilson ran the route from Liverpool to Australia for gold hunters seeking riches in the colony. Following their initial success, the company then purchased its first ship, a barque ship, or sailing vessel with three masts, named Iowa.

When Wilson's son-in-law James Chambers became a partner in the White Star Line company, they soon realized they needed newer, faster ships in orders to compete in the market for the long route to Australia. Around the same time, a young Thomas Henry Ismay, who had partnered with a retired ship captain, Phillip Nelson, was increasing his wealth and began purchasing shares in the White Star Line. By 1867, following a large debt to its bank and a bad merger, the White Star Line faced bankruptcy and an outdated, old fleet.

Above; During construction, Belfast, 15 April 1909,
Bird's eye view from the top of a gantry of
the triple-screw steamer.

With competitor Samuel Cunard's new steamship company securing immigrant trade, government and Royal Mail contracts, the White Star Line looked to be in real trouble. Ismay saw the opportunity to purchase the business at a low price and then began selling off the old ships while leasing and chartering new ones to start the business growth.

Accumulating capital, Ismay soon had the company running steamships under the White Star Line name and established a new company, the Oceanic Steam Navigation Company. Ismay held the controlling interest and established good working relationships with shareholders, including Gustuv Wolff and Edward Harland. Considered the highest priced shipbuilders in Europe, Harland and Wolff's shipbuilding company paid their craftsmen well and became successful based on their reputation for quality.

Under their new business partnership, the three were ambitious to build faster, stronger and higher quality iron ships. By working together and agreeing not to contract out to other companies, they focused on building to their own specifications and continued to invest in quality materials and labor.

Ismay set about revolutionizing the passenger trades by building with Harland and Wolff a quartet of vessels that were designed with comfort and passenger safety in mind. Previously, ships had not fully considered this either an asset or competitive advantage.

Ismay introduced first-class accommodations on new ships, with dining saloons and decks named promenades, running water and electricity. The very first ship to be constructed in this fashion was the Oceanic in 1899. Oceanic was committed to comfort and reliability rather than speed, which set it apart from the White Star Line's competitors and their ships.

Above; Cabin on the First Class deck.

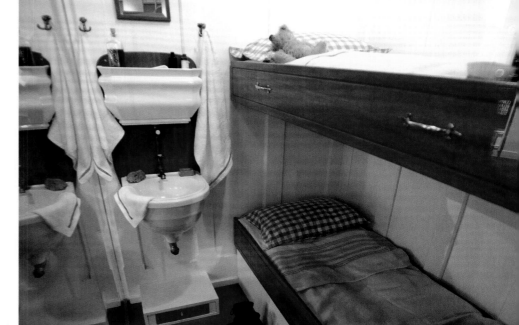

Below; A computer generated image shows the thi class accommodation available on the Titan

Main; : The RMS Oceanic, the second White Star liner to bear the name, circa 1908. She was launched in 1899 and ran aground in Shetland in 1914.

The White Star Line always kept its competition in mind. Because Cunard Line's ships were faster, White Star Line differentiated itself by offering luxuries to its passengers. Even third-class passengers received small luxuries such as privacy. In regular vessels, third-class travellers slept in open-berthed dormitories, which were usually located at the forward end of the vessel. The White Star Line segmented its accommodations into quarters for single men, which were much less crowded than their competitor's berths and into private two, four and six-berth cabins for single women, married couples and families in separate sections of the ship.

Interestingly, the American Immigration Commission ran a secret investigation into the travel conditions of immigrants aboard the ships and sent an undercover agent named Anna Herkner to travel on three different providers' ships. Records at Ellis Island reveal which ships she had included in her study.

In 1905, Herkner travelled aboard the North German Lloyd line's Friedrich Der Grosse, followed in 1907 by the Hamburg Amerika Line's Pennsylvania and in 1909, the White Star Line's Cedric. On the first two journeys she reported witnessing stewards making inappropriate and unwelcome sexual assaults on female passengers in third-class, a severe lack of medical care and extremely poor quality food. When Herkner travelled with the White Star Line, she described the shared cabin as private, comfortable and clean. With better quality food, open space on deck, private washbasins, the liner even offered additional modest luxuries such as clothing hooks and mirrors.

The third-class passenger accommodation aboard a White Star Line ship meant dining rooms served with linens and silverware, with menu cards that doubled as postcards and each ship featured a smoking and reading room for its third-class passengers as well as its first-class and second-class travellers.

By the early 1900s, the shipping companies were embroiled in a pricing war. The American financier John Pierpont Morgan, a railroad, coal and steel magnate, bought out White Star Line's entire rival shipping companies and established the trust named International Mercantile Marine (IMM).

Until 1901, RMS Oceanic was the largest ship in the world and became known as *'Queen of the Ocean'*. Ismay's policy was to use only the best materials and skilled workers for the construction of this new breed of liner. Accommodating over 1,700 passengers, the design focused on smooth lines and quality. Completely different from her competitors, Oceanic was the first ship to combine the hull and the superstructure, where other ships had added the superstructure to the deck. By incorporating them together, the deck was free for passengers to take in the view and the decking became known as the promenade.

Left; Edward Harland, founder of shipbuilders Harland & Wolff.

Main; Technical ship plans line the walls in the old Harland and Wolff Drawing Office in The Titanic Quarter, Belfast.

On Ismay's death, his son Joseph Bruce succeeded him in 1899. The new Harland and Wolff chairman Lord Pirrie had succeeded Harland on his death in 1895. The two new leaders formed a partnership. Between 1901 and 1907, the White Star Line purchased passenger liners Celtic, Cedric, Baltic and Adriatic. Dubbed 'The Big Four', they carried impressive numbers of passengers, as well as capacity for cargo. Instead of aiming to compete with Cunard Line on speed, the direction of the White Star Line's innovation for its new ships would be wholly focused on space, luxury and size.

White Star Line's timing for these enormous passenger liners was not entirely coincidental with regard to the emigration trend. Millions of Europeans were journeying to the United States and Canada to seek fortune in growing economies. Among the first to offer affordable accommodation for third-class passengers, White Star Line also sought to capture the luxury market by offering paying first and second-class accommodation.

These liners were more than doubling capacity for passengers and the company advertised comprehensively for immigrant passengers. Extending their operations from British and Irish immigrants, the company had seen success advertising and promoting its services to Scandinavia, Italy and Central Europe. Their routes included, Liverpool to New York, Montreal and Boston, Genoa and Southampton to New York, with each of these five separate routes offering major European stops along the way.

Above; The first class living room.

The White Star Line's quest for grandeur culminated in the design and build of the Titanic. Its lavish interior and luxurious details meant the interior was designed to make the liner more like a hotel than a ship. With even a barbershop and beauty salon, the liner carried every modern comfort and convenience for its passengers.

Titanic was commissioned to be the largest, fastest and most luxurious ocean liner in the world. It was a sign of progress and innovative Edwardian times.

Many of the Titanic's luxuries were a first in oceanic travel. A heated swimming pool was the first of its kind on board a passenger liner. In 1912, rooms featuring electric lighting and heating were in themselves considered luxuries. Impressive for its day and its size, the Titanic heated and lit all 840 rooms. The ship's manifest also showed it carried French staff to serve in the Parisian Café, which was an extra touch designed to impress its customers. The White Star Line went to great lengths to surprise and delight its passengers.

In line with its quest for the best, the shipping company paid its employees well. At the time of his employment as Captain of the Titanic, it was reported that Edward James Smith earned about the equivalent of $72,500 (£48,000) per year (by today's standards).

Travelling first-class on the Titanic was considered expensive – the ticket price matched the luxury and quality of the experience. First-class suite tickets were $4,350, which is roughly $18,000 (£12,000) by today's standards. A first-class berth, however, was $150 or $1724 (£1,130) by today's standards. Second-class cabin entry was $60 or $690 (£450) by today's standards. A third-class accommodation aboard Titanic was between $40 and $92 depending on the type or $172 (£113) and $460 (£302) by today's standards.

Main;; The Titanic swimming pool.

Shortly after the Titanic disaster, Ismay retired and resigned his position as chairman. As Ismay told the American inquiry into the Titanic's accident, he had put no cap or limit on the cost of either the Olympic or the Titanic, "All we ask them to do is to produce us the very finest ship they possibly can; the question of money has never been considered at all," he said.

"What do you think I am? Do you believe that I'm the sort that would have left that ship as long as there were any women and children on board? That's the thing that hurts and it hurts all the more because it is so false and baseless. I have searched my mind with deepest care, I have thought long over each single incident that I could recall of that wreck. I'm sure that nothing wrong was done; that I did nothing that I should not have done. My conscience is clear and I have not been a lenient judge of my own acts."

J. Bruce Ismay, Director of the White Star Line

Main; Joseph Bruce Ismay, chairman and son of the founder of the White Star Line.

Main; Officers of the White Star liner 'Olympic' including Lieutenant Murdoch (far left) and Captain John Smith (right) later captain of the ill-fated 'Titanic.'

LEADERSHIP AND LOYALTY

Captain & Crew

Viewed both heroically and critically for his actions as captain of the Titanic, Captain Edward John Smith perished with the ship he commanded. Born in Hanley, Stoke-on-Trent, England, Smith was the son of a pottery presser and grocer who rose to become *'the millionaire's captain'*. Working his way up the social ladder, Smith's first job out of school was operating a steam hammer and after three years went to sea with his half-brother who captained a sailing ship.

At 25, Smith passed his certificate of competency and went on to become regarded as one of the safest and most affable captains, leading and commanding some of the biggest ships of his time. He captained the Titanic's sister ship the Olympic and was the most senior of the White Star Line's captains.

Having worked for the White Star Line from 1880,

Smith was offered captaincy of the Majestic in 1895 and transported Boer War troops to Cape Colony. Having made two trips to South Africa without incident, he was awarded the Transport Medal by King Edward VII in 1903. His reputation as a safe captain grew with this accolade.

"When anyone asks me how I can best describe my experience of almost 40 years at sea, I merely say, uneventful. Of course there have been winter gales and storms and fog and the like. But in all my experience I have never been in any accident, or any sort worth speaking about. I have seen but one vessel in distress in all my years at sea. I never saw a wreck and never have been wrecked nor was I ever in any predicament that threatened to end in disaster of any sort."

Captain Edward J. Smith, 1907

Above; The Titanic, captained by Edward J. Smith

Main; First Class Dining Room of White Star Liner.

From 1904, Captain Smith commanded only the newest ships of the White Star Line on their maiden voyages. Smith had considered his retirement prior to accepting the captaincy of the Titanic, due to the time he had spent away from family with his career at sea. However, on the prestigious offer to command the world's largest passenger liner, the captain accepted and moved with his family to Southampton.

There are many myths still surrounding the captaincy of the Titanic, in the same way that there were myths about it being unsinkable. Many have reported the Captain's ignorance of ice warnings, although some historians since have said Smith did not necessarily ignore the warnings and given the weather was calm, it was not unusual for the captain to sail on into icy conditions at speed.

Smith's first four days captaining the liner reportedly went by trouble-free. He was said to have taken his meals at a small table in the dining saloon or in his cabin, which was attended by his valet.

*Above; A telegraph message from RMS Olympic, a sister ship to Titanic, reports that it has
received word from the Titanic that it has stuck an iceberg.*

The morning of 14th April 1912, Smith posted a message on the bridge that a warning was issued about ice. Smith then went on to lead the religious service for the first-class passengers, before returning to another message about dangerous ice from the Baltic. By early afternoon, Smith had shown Ismay the note, who had apparently held on to it.

At approximately 7pm that evening, the warning was posted on the bridge. Smith attended a private party held in his honour by Mr. and Mrs. George Dunton Widener in the a la carte restaurant, but excused himself early. Another warning about the icebergs from the nearby ship the Californian was then overheard by the Titanic crew.

After the dinner party, Smith met with his Second Officer, Charles Lightoller, who was keeping watch, on the bridge and discussed the temperature before retiring to bed. Following the collision, Smith was alerted and went to the bridge to assess it and upon learning the liner was sinking, ordered the crew to prepare the lifeboats.

Smith's body was never discovered. His wife and daughter were grief-stricken. A week after the tragedy, Smith's wife Sarah Eleanor Smith graciously wrote,

"To my poor fellow sufferers: My heart overflows with grief for you all and is laden with sorrow that you are weighed down with this terrible burden that has been thrust upon us. May God be with us and comfort us all."

Captain Smith was supported with approximately 885 crew members, who were not all permanent employees but, as was standard at the time, many were casual employees recruited especially for the voyage. Only a small crew served during the Titanic's sea trials; the crew numbers were bulked up for its maiden voyage.

*Main; Captain of White Star
Liner, RMS Titanic, Portrait of
Commander Edward J, Smith,
who died when Titanic sank on
15th April 1912.*

Previously Chief Mate of the Olympic with Captain Smith, Henry Tingle Wilde also came across to the Titanic. In what was dubbed the 'officer reshuffle', Smith and Wilde took over the top jobs while the ship's previously designated Chief Mate and First Officer, William McMaster Murdoch and Charles Lightoller, were given the ranks of First and Second Officer.

Chief Mate or Officer Wilde was born in Liverpool and, like Smith, spent his teenage years sailing and joined White Star Line after passing his masters certificate. While he was second-in-command to Smith on the Olympic, the ship collided with HMS Hawke in 1911. He was originally due to board the Olympic again the week before Titanic sailed, but the day before he was included as second-in-charge to Smith on the liner's maiden voyage.

Along with First Officer Murdoch, Wilde did not survive the disaster. Murdoch and Lightoller were competent officers although there were obvious concerns regarding their seniority aboard the Titanic, having had the demotions right before the journey. It was Murdoch who had apparently received the message from the Sixth Officer James Moody regarding the call from the lookouts warning of the iceberg.

Murdoch ordered the helm hard to port in order to try to avoid the iceberg, but it was too late. Murdoch had also attempted to save as many lives as possible by ordering them into lifeboats. The ranks of the remaining officer crew supporting Smith included Third Officer Herbert John Pitman who had tried to encourage more frightened passengers aboard the lifeboats. He watched the Titanic sink and was one of those who claimed to have witnessed it sink whole.

*Above; A group of survivors from the 'Titanic' disaster arrive at Liverpool on the 'Adriatic'.
3rd officer Herbert John Pitman stands on the right (wearing a cap). 11th May 1912.*

Fourth Officer Joseph Groves Boxhall survived the Titanic's disaster, along with Fifth Officer Harold Godfrey Lowe. Lowe was not on duty when the ship collided with the iceberg and reports were he was asleep and woke to find the rescue underway. Lowe infamously had a disagreement with Ismay who had instructed Lowe and the seaman to *"Lower away!"*, at which Lowe reportedly responded "You want me to lower away quickly? You'll have me drown the lot of them!" After lowering a number of lifeboats, Sixth Officer Moody then instructed Lowe to go on the next boat. Moody had said to Lowe he would find another lifeboat later but he did not survive.

The Titanic's crew was then divided into three principal departments, Deck, Engine and Victualling. On deck, there were 66 crew members; the engine had 325 and victualling 494 staff. It was reported that the majority of the crewmen were not necessarily seamen and held skills as engineers, firemen or stokers. Only 23 of the crew were women and were mainly stewardesses.

To manage and service the many facilities on board, the White Star Line employed bakers, chefs, butchers, stewards, gymnasium instructors, laundrymen, waiters, bed-makers, fishmongers, dishwashers and cleaners. There was even a printer on board who received the latest news from the wireless and produced a daily newspaper titled the Atlantic Daily Bulletin.

Some subcontractors, for the Royal Mail and the United States Post Office Department, were also considered crew, along with the staff of the First Class A La Carte Restaurant and the Café Parisien. There were also radio operators employed by Marconi and the eight musicians, who were employed by an agency. According to reports, they travelled as second-class passengers.

Above; W. Hartley, the leader of the Titanic's band of eight musicians and one of the many men that died at their post when the ship sank.

Above; Members of the ship's crew in their life jackets.

Carrying seniority over other crew members, the Titanic also employed 29 Able Seamen and an Able Officer, who had additional skills and training and were capable of operating the lifeboats and the lifeboat davits. Two Boatswain Mates managed the deck cranes winches and lines. The Able Seamen team had six lookouts, who worked two at a time in two-hour shifts. Ordinarily, the lookouts would have used binoculars, although on the maiden voyage for some reason they were locked away. Facing a 20-mile-per-hour headwind and darkness, it was arguable how reliable binoculars would have been even if they had been used. Seven quartermasters were also Able Seamen who worked on the bridge to steer the ship and manage signal flags and navigation.

Of the Engine Crew, there were 25 engineers and 10 electricians and boilermakers. The highest paid of all the crew, the engineers were in charge of maintaining the engines, generators and mechanical equipment.

One story of an Irish crew member surfaced long after the Titanic's sinking. Assistant deck engineer, 33-year-old Thomas Millar, worked at Harland and Wolff as an engine fitter and had helped build the engines of Olympic and Titanic. Following the death of his wife, Jeannie, in January 1912, Millar decided to bring his two young children to America and settle there.

After he left Belfast on the Titanic, the children were left in the care of an aunt in a village, after which he had planned on returning to them, to meet them either in Queenstown or Southampton in order to board a ship themselves. At age 11 and five, Millar gave his boys two new pennies each before he boarded the Titanic. He had reportedly told them not to spend them until his return.

Sadly, Millar did not survive, his body was never recovered and the boys were left orphaned. Their aunt raised them in Ireland. Thomas Millar's name is included on the Titanic Memorial, Belfast City Hall. Youngest son, William Ruddick Millar, did not spend the pennies given to him and, according to reports; they remain with the Millar family to this day.

The night of the Titanic's disaster the Second Engineering Officer, James Hesketh and Leading Fireman Fred Barrett were inspecting the coalbunker where a fire had broken out not long after the ship first set sail. When the Titanic collided with the iceberg at 11.40pm, the ship was damaged by the iceberg in this particular section, which is where the men were inspecting the progress with eliminating the fire. They escaped to the Number 5 Boiler Room and closed the bulkhead doors.

Of the firemen onboard, there were 13 leaders called Stoker Foremen and 163 firemen named Stokers. With 29 boilers, each fireman was assigned one boiler and three furnaces. Within the six boiler rooms, 10-15 firemen were assigned to a Stoker Foreman. The shifts for this crew were incredibly demanding. Working in 49 degree Celsius heat (120F) the men worked four hours on and eight hours off.

Determined by some historians the worst crew role on the ship, Coal Trimmers were employed to work inside the coal bunkers which were very close to the boilers. Using shovels and wheelbarrows to keel the coal level, there were 73 trimmers who worked on the Titanic, of whom it is reported 20 survived.

Above; A pair of binoculars from the RMS Titanic.

Main; Titanic's engineers, including 14 of the lost officers.

Main; The boilers of the White Star liner Olympic.

Working in the engine rooms alongside the engineers, 33 Greasers were responsible for maintaining oil and lubricants for the mechanical equipment. In total, 244 engineers, firemen, trimmers and greasers lost their lives when the Titanic sank.

Of the 421 Victualling crew, 322 were stewards servicing the dining rooms, public rooms, cabins and other facilities. 62 Victualling crew were employed in the galley and kitchen, as cooks, chefs, bakers, butchers and dishwashers (then called scullions).

Above; Part of the engines.

The memoirs of one of Titanic's female stewardesses tell the story of her journeys on the sea. Starting on the Olympic, Violet Jessop described the silk furnishings and lush interiors. When Olympic collided with HMS Hawke, she was on board.

Above; The lifeboats.
All that was left of the greatest ship in the world.

Above; The First Class gymnasium on board the Titanic.

Main; First class smoking room on the Olympic White Star liner, c 1911.

Above; The Titanic Survivors Were Picked up by the Carpathia.

Then, remarkably she also survived the Titanic's collision and sinking. She had joined as a stewardess on the largest cruise liner and described it as the grandest of ships. It was improved in every way – lace bedspreads were described as truly beautiful. She heard the crash and went down to get life jackets and in her account described the mess and personal effects scattered everywhere. A mason threw a baby to Jessop asking her to mind it, in the middle of the chaos that followed. Unbelievably, Jessop survived a third ocean liner disaster while working as a nurse on the HMS Britannic after the surviving the Titanic. Jessop passed away in 1971.

Above; Titanic life-preserver, which was worn by Titanic survivor Miss Mabel Francatelli.

LORDS, LADIES AND GENTLEMEN

The Passengers

When Ismay and Pirrie came together to dream up the world's largest ship, they were ambitious for luxury too and with the upper class' access to disposable wealth, there was a great market for luxury travel. Both the British and American elite were aboard the Titanic on that fateful first journey.

With silent film stars mixing with entrepreneurs and the English upper classes, it must have been a fascinating scene in the austere, refined dining room. Indeed, for those first-class passengers aboard the liner, it was like staying in a rather large luxury hotel. With elegant double first-class suites, library, a la carte restaurant and promenades, it offered all the beautiful scenery of a fine hotel with the added excitement of views over a vast ocean.

Of the first-class set, there were fascinating characters aboard. The upper class passengers included businessmen, industrialists and bankers.

The most famous of American first-class passengers on the Titanic, Margaret Brown, whose nickname was Molly, became famous for surviving the disaster and earned the title "*The Unsinkable Molly Brown*". A socialite and philanthropist, Brown was born to Irish Catholic immigrants in Missouri. At 18, after moving to Colorado with her sister, she married James Joseph Brown, a self-taught miner with entrepreneurial spirit who came from nothing to create a wealthy mining and engineering career for himself. Following the birth of two children, Brown became involved in the women's suffragette movement and grew to be well-known in society circles, learning the arts and to speak fluent French, German and Russian.

Brown also ran for Senate twice and was active in fundraising circles. She and her husband separated amicably and quietly, with Brown supported by a substantial cash settlement, home and monthly allowance. They remained friends until his death.

It was reported that Brown was travelling across Europe when she had word her first grandchild was ill and had decided to depart for New York on the next available ship, the Titanic.

*Above; A photograph of passengers using
'cycle racing machines' in the gymnasium.*

Main; Janet Kalstrom, playing Molly Brown, John Steinle, middle, playing Captain Edward John Smith, captain of the Titanic and Mary Van Meter, a docent at the museum, reenacted the day of the sinking of the Titanic to a roomful of visitors.

Brown earned her Titanic title reportedly because of her heroic behaviour. She had helped others board the lifeboats before herself and was finally convinced to get in Lifeboat Number 6. Once safe on the lifeboat, Brown took an oar and tried to row back to save more people from the water, but was told by the crewman, Quartermaster Robert Hichens, that if they did go back they would either be sucked down with the wreck or those in the water would overwhelm the boat. Brown and the other women took turns rowing to keep warm and to keep their spirits up. The story remains unsubstantiated, like so many Titanic stories, as some determine they did return to rescue more people and some determining they did not.

After her survival, she worked to help other survivors and helped establish the Survivors' Committee, was elected as Chair and raised $10,000 for survivors who had lost everything and were destitute. Remaining till all survivors had met with family members, friends or had received medical help, Brown later helped erect a memorial for the Titanic in Washington DC.

Her story became such a source of fascination that a musical and movie were made based on her life. Much later, so much myth and legend was attached to Brown's life and story that her family tired of public attention. The first full-length biography of Brown, by Kristen Iversen *Molly Brown: Unravelling the Myth*, that has been substantiated by family members and Brown's letters and scrapbooks was published in 1999.

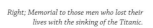

Right; Memorial to those men who lost their lives with the sinking of the Titanic.

The richest known person travelling the Titanic was multi-millionaire John Jacob Astor IV. Astor was travelling with his wife, Madeleine, who was his second wife and was five months pregnant.

An American businessman who had a portfolio of varied interests, including real estate, inventing and writing, Astor was also considered the richest man in the world at the time he embarked the Titanic. Astor was a talented man, having written a science fiction novel about life on other planets in the year 2000, titled *A Journey in Other Worlds*. He also invented a bicycle brake and helped develop a turbine engine that was patented. He most famously built the Astoria Hotel in New York City, which became the Waldorf-Astoria as it adjoined his cousin's Waldorf Hotel.

From a prominent family in the US, he was closely linked with the Roosevelt family. After Astor scandalously divorced his first wife, with whom he had two children, Astor again shocked the society set by announcing his marriage at 47-years to an 18-year-old Madeleine. Madeleine was a year younger than his son.

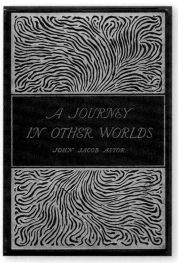

Above; A Journey in Other Worlds by John Jacob Astor.

Main; Waldorf Astoria Hotel, New York.

Main; Passengers boarding the Titanic Special train at Waterloo Station to Southampton.

The newly wed Astors were travelling as part of an extended honeymoon, likely to escape the high society gossip and discovered Madeleine was pregnant when they decided to travel back to the US by the Titanic in time for the baby's arrival.

According to reports, when the collision occurred and for some time after, Astor was very calm. When he helped his wife, her maid and nurse into lifeboat A shortly before 2am, he apparently asked to join her because of her pregnancy. He was last seen smoking and went down with the ship half an hour later. What actually happened in that last hour of his life is not exactly known. Some reports tell the story of Astor willingly giving up his position in the lifeboat to offer it to a young immigrant who was nearby. Other accounts tell of his helping his wife in the lifeboat, kissing her and returning to the deck.

Sadly, his wife and baby survived but he did not. Madeleine returned to New York and four months later to the day gave birth to John Jacob Astor VI. A newspaper article from 1916 claimed she lived a secluded life mourning the loss of her husband, until she re-married four years later.

Another first-class gentleman travelling on the Titanic was Benjamin Guggenheim, who also was lost during the tragedy. Guggenheim was another American businessman who inherited a mining fortune from his father. He was estranged from his wife and was travelling the Titanic with his mistress, a French singer Leontine Aubert, while his wife and family were at home in New York.

After his maid and personal valet woke the couple from sleep and when the maid and Aubert were safe in Lifeboat No 9, Guggenheim and his valet understood they would not be rescued. The legend of this businessman's passing was fantastic: he apparently encouraged his valet to change into evening attire and the two men drank brandy and smoked cigars under the Grand Staircase, saying *"We've dressed up in our best and are prepared to go down like gentlemen."*

He was reported to have given two further messages to his wife, one to a survivor who relayed his first, *"Tell my wife, if it should happen that my secretary and I both go down, tell her I played the game straight to the end. No woman shall be left aboard this ship because Benjamin Guggenheim was a coward."* And finally writing, *"If anything should happen to me, tell my wife I've done my best in doing my duty."*

Main; Florette Guggenheim (nee Seligman 1870 - 1937, right) and her brother James de Witt Seligman at the offices of the White Star shipping line in New York, April 1912. The pair are waiting to enquire about the welfare of Guggenheim's husband, American businessman Benjamin Guggenheim, who was a passenger on board the Titanic when she sank on 15th April. Benjamin Guggenheim was not among the survivors.

Above; Lady Duff-Gordon.

Of the British first-class passengers, there were some interesting and controversial characters aboard. Sir Cosmo and Lady Duff-Gordon were prominent members of British society. Lady Duff-Gordon was a notable dress designer who boasted a wealthy and elite clientele, including Oscar Wilde and the British royal family. She was a divorcee, controversially and even worse, her sister allegedly wrote erotica fiction. They married in 1910. Sir Duff-Gordon was a well-known Scottish landowner and sportsman who inherited his title from his great uncle for his contribution to the Crown during the Peninsular War. An Olympic fencer, Duff-Gordon earned notoriety for the circumstances surrounding his survival of the Titanic disaster. Rescued in Lifeboat Number 1, along with his wife and secretary, the couple survived and was later asked to testify at The British Board of Trade's inquiry regarding the nature of their rescue.

Because they had boarded a lifeboat that had a capacity of 40 and there were only 12 people on board, Sir Duff-Gordon was criticized for boarding in opposition of the women and children first policy and for failing to rescue people struggling in the freezing water.

It was rumored that he had bribed the lifeboat crew not to rescue more from the water. This went unsubstantiated and the inquiry accepted his denial of this claim. The couple had also stated that there were no other women and children waiting to board the lifeboat, which matched eyewitness accounts that First Officer Murdoch offered them places on the lifeboat. The inquiry still concluded the lifeboat could have rescued more people, however.

Isidor (Isador) Straus was another famous passenger with a first-class ticket. Straus was the co-owner of Macy's department store in New York after opening a crockery department as part of their china and crockery import business. Straus and his wife, Ida, were a devoted couple and famously would not part ways for the rescue following the Titanic's collision.

Having travelled back from Europe, when the ship they had journeyed on looked to be sinking, Ida refused to leave her husband, declining to get into a lifeboat. He was then offered a seat to accompany her but would not go while there were still women and children left. Another Titanic survivor reported the two would not separate, with Straus not leaving before other men, women and children and Ida refusing to leave her husband. Other witnesses recalled Ida said, *"I will not be separated from my husband. As we have lived, so will we die together."*

Below; Isidor Straus (1845 - 1912), co-owner of the Macy's department store.

Main; The second-class promenade on the boat deck

Above; Computer video projections of passengers are displayed in a recreation of a second class cabin at the Titanic Belfast visitor attraction

Second-class passengers included authors, clergymen and holidaymakers. For those travelling second-class on the Titanic, their experience was not too dissimilar to what many first-class passengers would enjoy on other liners. The standard of luxury on the Titanic was so high, even the second-class passengers had the convenience of an elevator. This was another Titanic first.

An English public school teacher, Lawrence Beesley was travelling to America for a holiday. A scholar and prizeman at Caius College, Cambridge, he took a first class in science and went on to teach at a grammar school and then became a science master.

Beesley wrote, "*When arranging a tour around the United States I had decided to cross on the Titanic. It was rather a novelty to be on the largest ship yet launched. It was no exaggeration to say that it was quite easy to lose one's way on such a ship.*"

While in his second-class cabin, Beesley noticed the heave in the engine on collision and asked a steward what had happened. While they said nothing, he reported feeling a strange sensation walking back up the stairs – as if his feet did not fall where they should. When he arrived on Deck A, men were being allowed to board lifeboats and at 1.25am he boarded Lifeboat Number 13. On being lowered down, the lifeboat very nearly had an accident of its own.

"

As I dressed, I heard the order shouted, 'All the passengers on deck with life belts on.' We all walked up slowly with the life belts tied on over our clothing, but even then we presumed that this was merely a wise precaution the captain was taking. The ship was absolutely still and except for the gentle, almost unnoticeable, tilt downwards, there were no visible signs of the approaching disaster. But, in a few moments, we saw the covers being lifted from the boats and the crews allotted to them standing by and uncoiling the ropes, which were to lower them. We then began to realize that it was a more serious matter than we had at first supposed. Presently we heard the order, 'All men stand back away from the boats. All ladies retire to the next deck below.' The men all stood away and waited in absolute silence, some leaning against the end railings of the deck, others pacing slowly up and down. The boats were level with the deck where all the women were collected, the women got in quietly, with the exception of some, who refused to leave their husbands. In some cases they were torn from their husbands and pushed into the boats, but in many instances they were allowed to remain, since there was no-one to insist that they should go.

"

Beesley wrote of his experience in _The Loss of the SS Titanic_, which went on to become a highly successful book.

Above; Some of the fortunate passengers in the life-boats alongside the sinking vessel.

Main; How the Titanic Survivors Were Picked up by the Carpathia.

Of the second-class aboard, many were maids or servants to first-class passengers. Charles Aldworth, a chauffeur to William Carter in first-class, was a 30-year-old single man who embarked the Titanic, along with his Renault automobile. He was the only member of Carter's entourage who travelled second-class, the others all taking a first-class ticket. He did not survive.

Of the children aboard, along with women they had priority of rescue. Eva Hart and her mother were among them. Travelling to America in second-class, Hart was only seven years old when her parents Be njamin and Esther boarded at Southampton. Hart's mother did not trust the Titanic was unsinkable and feared sleeping while they journeyed at night.

She said of her mother's 'premonition': *"my mother said to my father that she had made up her mind quite firmly that she would not go to bed in that ship, she would sit up at night. She decided that she wouldn't go to bed at night and she didn't!"*

Hart was woken by her father shortly after the collision and was taken to the boat's deck, where he put Hart and her mother in Lifeboat Number 14. Hart recalls the last words from her father were *"hold mummy's hand and be a good girl"*.

Below ; Lifeboats on board the SS Titanic.

Main; Artist's conception of ocean liner Titanic plunging beneath the waves, as survivors in lifeboats watch.

Hart never saw her father again. Suffering from nightmares and vivid recollections, Hart said much later in an interview,

"I saw that ship sink. I never closed my eyes. I didn't sleep at all. I saw it, I heard it and nobody could possibly forget it. I can remember the colors, the sounds, everything. The worst thing I can remember are the screams."

Hart was involved in conventions and anniversaries of the Titanic and wrote an autobiography *Shadow of the Titanic – A Survivor's Story*. She was outspoken about how the ship sank, in two pieces, about how too few lifeboats there were and about how close the SS Californian was, which failed to rescue the Titanic passengers.

Above; The violin of Wallace Hartley, long thought to have been either lost at sea or stolen. As far as Titanic memorabilia goes, it is one of the most important pieces that has ever been found.

Not quite a child, the 15-year-old Edith Brown was another well-known second-class passenger who survived the Titanic. Brown's father, a hotel owner, was opening a new hotel business in Washington, USA and booked his wife and daughter tickets. Her father had also bought on board and stored in the Titanic's hold tableware, furnishings and bed linen for the new hotel. Brown recalled the Titanic's incident in interviews and in her biography *A Lifetime on the Titanic*. Her father never survived, she recalled her and her mother's rescue,

"Father appeared a few minutes later. He told us, 'You'd better put on your life jackets and something warm, it's cold on deck. It's just a precaution. We've struck an iceberg, it's nothing much. The steward in the corridor says it's nothing to worry about.' We waited for ages on the boat deck for someone to tell us what to do. The ship's band was playing ragtime. They played to keep our spirits up. Everybody kept saying: 'She's unsinkable. She won't go down. Father kissed us and saw us into Lifeboat 14. Up to fifty people got in as it swung perilously over the side. One man jumped into the boat dressed as a woman. As we rowed away from the ship, we could still hear the band playing, but now it was hymns. We were almost six hours in the lifeboat and during that time we had no water and nothing to eat. I kept wondering if my father had got off the ship, that's all I could think of."

After passing away aged 100, Brown was the longest-living survivor of the Titanic.

Right; W. Woodward, a member of the Titanic's band of eight musicians and one of the many men that died at their post when the ship sank on 15th April 1912, The band played on until the water was over their feet.

Of the passengers travelling third-class (also called steerage), there were more than 30 nationalities, many of whom were immigrants to the US. There were reportedly 120 Irish passengers, over 60 Finnish, over 20 Belgians and many more making up the more than 700 aboard who were looking to make a fresh, new start in the 'new world' in the US and Canada. There were reports of mothers travelling alone with young children to join their husbands already working in America.

Lillian Asplund was five years old when she and her family were third-class passengers. She remembered that the Titanic was very big, had been freshly painted and that she did not like the smell of the paint.

Born in Massachusetts to a Swedish family, her father had taken his family to Sweden after his own father had died, in order to assist his mother.

On wishing to return his family to the US, Asplund and her four brothers joined her parents on the Titanic. After disaster struck, her father had the family join Lifeboat Number 15. She later said, *"my*

mother said she would rather stay with him [my father] and go down with the ship, but he said the children should not be alone. [My mother] had Felix on her lap and she had me between her knees. I think she thought she could keep me a little warmer that way."

Asplund lost her father and two of her brothers. She was reported to have described the ship sinking as similar to a large building going down. Asplund followed her mother's guidance and hardly talked of the tragedy. The occasion that she did talk publicly of the experience, she described looking up and seeing the faces of her father and brothers peering through the rails, which haunted her. She kept her Titanic ticket until death, after which it was auctioned.

Above; Funeral for the last American survivor of the Titanic, Lillian Gertrud Asplund.

Left; Immigrants boarding the White Star Liner Titanic at Queenstown (Cobh), Ireland, for the ship's maiden voyage.

Above; Men and women hugging as crew members direct women and children (both in life jackets, along with some crewmen) to lifeboats following an accident.

Another family travelling third-class was Frederick Goodwin's. Travelling with his wife Augusta and six children, William, Charles, Harold, Lillian, Jessie and baby Sidney, Goodwin was relocating from England to New York for a new job at a power plant. Sadly, the whole family died when the ship sank.

Of the children in third-class, not many stories are known, with the exception of nine-year-old Frank Goldsmith. Goldsmith's father was a toolmaker and was taking his wife and child to Detroit, Michigan.

While on board, Goldsmith recalled playing with other third-class boys, climbing and playing, watching the stokers at work in the engine room. Goldsmith later wrote a book on his Titanic experience, *Echoes in the Night*.

He recalled, *"My dad reached down and patted me on the shoulder and said, 'So long, Frankie, I'll see you later.' He didn't and he may have known he wouldn't."*

SETTING SAIL

The Maiden Voyage

With four decades of experience at sea, Captain Smith was considered the White Star Line's most capable, safe, experienced and senior of their captains.

On the Titanic's maiden voyage, it was under capacity, which was unexpected for the standard of vessel and the prestige of joining the first journey. Because of a coal strike in Britain at the time, there were changes to travel plans and the ship could have accommodated hundreds more passengers. Exact numbers of passengers aboard are debated even today, as not all passengers collected and kept tickets and some cancelled or simply did not show on the day. The vessel was not affected by the coal strike for fuel, it had received coal from other liners at Southampton and stored at the dock.

Right; Edward John Smith (1850–1912).

"My mother had a premonition and she never went to bed in that ship at night at all. She sat up for three nights so she slept during the day and I was with my father. So my memories are of being with him and you know, father's spoiled little girl and playing and being in a nursery and meeting a lot of other children and generally enjoying myself. But right inside still thinking of how odd it was that my mother was never up during the day."

Eva Hart, Titanic Survivor

THE "GREAT UNSINKABLE" TITANIC.

The largest and most luxurious vessel ever designed by man. The Queen of the Ocean, in man's estimation unsinkable, struck an iceberg on Sunday, April 14th, 1912, at 11.45 p.m., and sank at 2.22 a.m., April 15th, with upwards of 1,500 souls. It is reported that as she was sinking the band played "Nearer my God to Thee."

Nothing solid, nothing certain,
Danger in each step we take;

The strongest ship that man can fashion,
God can in a moment break.

Above; A Titanic postcard signed by survivors Eva Hart, Bertam and Millvina Dean and Beatrice Sandstrom.

Above; A second class ticket from the RMS Titanic Star Line.

The coal loading was still being completed on the morning of the vessel's maiden voyage. Allegedly, in the hurry to load enough coal for the Titanic, there was not enough time for the crew to wet it down, which was standard practice. The coal was wetted to prevent fires and as dry coal and the dust generated, were fire hazards, a fire broke out in Boiler Room Number 6. It was not unusual for fires generated from coal to be burning while ships sailed during this period, but the crew had to fight this particular fire throughout the maiden voyage.

It was not considered serious, or strong enough to warrant any concern and did not give the crew concern for damage to the ship.

While the sister ships the Olympic and the Titanic were registered with Liverpool as their home port and the offices of the White Star Line remained in Liverpool, the Olympic class liners were to sail out of Southampton because of its convenience to London. It also had an easy journey across the English Channel to gain customers from Europe. Most liners used this route following the Olympic class.

Above; Liners in Southampton Dock. Photographed during the Titanic's departure, on her maiden voyage to New York.

Main; Miners emerging from a tunnel at a colliery for the last time during the coal strike crisis.

The White Star Line had ambitiously planned out voyages for the Olympic, with Titanic also using this route and had worked on schedules for weekly sailings. It was not destined to be following the disastrous maiden voyage of the Titanic.

Of the maiden voyage accounts and stories, there are many myths surrounding the occasion. It was said there was a cursed Egyptian mummy on board, a fable that gathered so much momentum the mummy was dubbed *'shipwrecker'*. There is no record or proof of a mummy in the Titanic's manifest of cargo loaded. It seems the story came about from a journalist who talked of a mummy on display in the British Museum, apparently at a dinner party.

Another unsubstantiated story attached to the launch and maiden voyage of the Titanic was a tale of a champagne bottle refusing to break on christening the ship. In fact, the White Star Line had a policy not to christen its ships with champagne, so the story surrounding the so-called *'bad luck'* of the unbroken bottle is untrue.

In addition, it was said a significant number of notable passengers had premonitions of a disaster related to the Titanic and had cancelled their trip accordingly. This was also a myth. Some passengers did cancel, but they were not for any kind of premonition. One passenger, for example, had sprained an ankle. It was reported that 55 bookings were cancelled.

*Above; Nearly the length of three football fields Titanic was, at
the time, the largest moving object ever created.*

*Main; Southampton Quayside. Crowd on the
Ocean Dock as seen from The Titanic.*

Crowds of people had gathered, along with members of the press, to inspect the huge ship and watch it take off on its maiden voyage. The Board of Trade was present to inspect and declare the ship fit for sailing. As part of this final inspection, two of the lifeboats were lowered to demonstrate they were functional and the crew was able to use them. There were also said to be tours of the ship held before the passengers began boarding.

*Above; Board of trade inspector examining lifebelts
on Titanic at Southampton.*

The passengers commenced boarding at 9.30 am, with third-class passengers the first to be invited on. During an hour and a half boarding process for these third-class passengers, in accordance with immigration regulations, they underwent a medical examination. This was to ensure American immigration would not decline passengers' entry by being declared medically unfit.

Second-class travellers had stewards escort them to their cabins and first-class passengers boarded last, each personally greeted by Captain Smith.

Above; Second Class Passengers boarding . The crew are wearing White Star jumpers.

*bove; A salvaged Third Class porthole
*om the wreck of the Titanic.

Above; An American doctor performs health checks, including symptoms
of glaucoma, on immigrants at point of departure.

*Main; Post ard of British luxury liner
S.S. Titanic in dock at Southampton*

S.S. TITANIC.
IN DOCK AT SOUTHAMPTON.

One of the survivors of the Titanic described the boarding of the ship after it sank. Roberta Maioni was a maid to the Countess of Rothes, who also survived.

"The weather was brilliant and the docks at Southampton were crowded with bustling people. For this was no ordinary boat departure; it was the departure of a wonder ship – a floating palace that far excelled all others in size and magnificence and men said that she could not sink.

We passengers were crushed and pushed about by excited crowds as we struggled to reach the gangway, but once across we were swallowed up in that great vessel.

The noise made in getting the luggage aboard was deafening, but when the Titanic started on its journey an even greater pandemonium broke loose – the cheering of thousands of people and the shrieking of many sirens."

Above; The Countess of Rothes, who was saved from the Titanic.

Above; Officers of the White Star liner 'Olympic' including Lieutenant Murdoch (far left) and Captain John Smith (right) later captain of the ill-fated 'Titanic.'

In addition to the first, second and third-class passengers who boarded the ship at Southampton on Wednesday 10th April 1912, the White Star Line's Ismay and designer Andrews, embarked to review the ship's performance. The owner of the liner Morgan was also meant to join, but had cancelled last minute.

The crew aboard the Titanic were expected early, with records of them boarding stating 5.18am onwards. Not all the crew arrived in time, however, and some crew members were fortunately late boarding the Titanic and missed certain death. More crew members, who were ready on standby, replaced them.

Main; Members of the ship's crew in their life jackets.

Main; Postcard of the Titanic, broadside view.

Main; First class dining saloon.

Of the crew joining, there have been messages and letters revealing their thoughts before sailing. One steward from Cornwall, Harry Bristow, who did not survive the Titanic's disaster, had written a letter to his wife the day before embarking, which read:

"Dear Et [Ethel], I have earned my first day's pay on the Titanic and been paid and I may say spent it, do you know dearie. I Forgot about towels, also cloth brush so I've to buy two. My uniform will cost £1 17s 6d, coat plus waistcoat and cap and star regulation collars and paper front (don't laugh dearie, it's quite true) to white jackets etc, so it won't leave me very much to take up. My pay is £3 15s plus tips. I'm in the first-class saloon so I may pick up a bit. I've been scrubbing the floor today in saloon, about a dozen of us. I lost myself a time or two, she is such an enormous size I expect it will take me a couple of trips before I begin to know my way about here. I believe we're due back here again about the 4th next month. I am not sure though. I've to be aboard about tomorrow morning 6 o'clock sharp, means turning out at 5am. You might send a letter to me addressed as envelope enclosed a day before we're expected in so that I could have it directly I come ashore, now dearie with fondest love to boy and self and be brave as you always are, your ever loving Harry."

Above; Portrait of three of the surviving crewmen from the RMS Titanic, among them, Frederick Dent Ray (left) and two other stewards, 1912.

Above; The 'New York' swinging towards the 'Titanic', resulting in near collision.

On departing Southampton, Captain Smith walked to the bridge and had his First Officer confirm the tugboats were ready to pull the liner out from the wharf. Apparently, he then said to him, *"Take her to sea Mr. Murdoch."*

The flag that signals departure, the Blue Peter, was raised on the Titanic and after messages were relayed between the officers and captain, Smith gave the first of three toots from the Titanic's whistle.

Leaving Southampton on time, at noon, the Titanic only narrowly missed an accident soon after. After five tugboats (named Ajax, Hector, Hercules, Vulcan and Neptune) pulled the huge liner along Southampton Water and the Titanic's giant propellers were set in motion, there was a close

call. The massive water displacement caused by the Titanic meant that as the liner passed the moored SS City of New York and Oceanic, the cables holding them were severely strained. While the Oceanic's mooring was not ultimately disturbed, the New York's cables were snapped and it began to swing dangerously near the Titanic.

The SS New York turned around toward the Titanic and almost collided. The New York was towed away by the tugboat the Vulcan, at just four feet from the Titanic. This near miss and subsequent rescue by the Vulcan caused a delay in departure for an hour.

Main; The Titanic aided by four tugs preparing to leave for Southampton for her maiden voyage.

*Main; The 'New York' being pushed
away from the Titanic by tugs.*

The incident did not go unnoticed and British newspapers eagerly reported on the moment.

"The departure of the Titanic on her maiden voyage on Wednesday was marred by an untoward incident which caused considerable consternation among the hundreds of people gathered on the quay-side to witness the sailing of the largest vessel afloat. By some means or other the passing of the Titanic caused the New York to break away from her position alongside the Oceanic with the results that the Titanic and the New York narrowly missed colliding with each other. Fortunately, the captain of the tug Vulcan was able to take a rapid glance of the situation and by his promptness and skill in manoeuvring he was able to hold the New York whilst the Titanic got clear and a very dangerous episode ended with nothing more than a few broken ropes."

Southampton Times and Hampshire Express, 13th April 1912

*Above; Banking and mining millionaire
Benjamin Guggenheim, father of Peggy Guggenheim.
He died when the liner, Titanic sank.*

"All eyes were fixed on the New York. It looked as if there must be a collision; but, as a matter of fact, there was no real danger. The Titanic's screws were stopped almost instantaneously and the New York was towed to safety. Then the Titanic slowly sped down Southampton Water, the faces of her passengers peering at every nook of the seven tiers along the whole length of the liner, until she melted away in the distance and her maiden voyage had begun."

The Standard, 10th April 1912

Heading out of the English Channel and passing the Isle of Wight, the Titanic made it safely through the tides and the Southampton waters. Headed for the first stop, the French port Cherbourg, the vessel had 77 nautical miles to travel. The passenger liner easily made the trip in four hours. With close to another 300 passengers joining the vessel, the passenger liner was still one hour behind schedule. Being too large to dock in Cherbourg, which was a deep water port, the passengers and luggage had to be ferried to the liner by two specially built 'tenders' named Traffic and Nomadic. The former was constructed to carry third-class passengers and the latter for first and second-class passengers. Of the 300 who joined the Titanic at Cherbourg, close to half were first-class passengers, including Benjamin Guggenheim and Sir Cosmo and Lady Duff-Gordon.

Almost one and a half hours later, the Titanic departed again, this time for Queenstown in Ireland. Arriving at Cork Harbour on the south coast of Ireland the next day at 11.30am, tenders or ferries again had to be used to bring passengers aboard. The dock facilities were not capable of managing a ship this size either. Having been moored approximately two miles offshore, the Titanic used Traffic and Nomadic to ferry the passengers, along with over 1300 bags of mail to be shipped to America.

As was the case at Cherbourg, some fortunate passengers left the vessel at this port, avoiding the tragedy to come. Among the departures were local Queenstown firemen and stoker John Coffey, who snuck off by hiding in mailbags offloaded to shore. Another fortunate departure was Father Francis Browne, who took a series of photographs on his short journey aboard the fated ship and took the last ever known photograph of the Titanic.

Two hours later, the Titanic had weighed anchor and moved into the North Atlantic Ocean, where the crew established a shift routine to manage watches and responsibilities. Captain Smith was aware of reports of ice, coming from the trade press in the weeks and months before setting sail.

Travelling in good time, speeding west toward what should have been the next and final port of call in New York, the Titanic followed the Irish coast for some 55 nautical miles and then sailed 1,620 nautical miles along a Great Circle route across the North Atlantic. The first three days of the voyage went uneventfully. In fact, in the first day of sailing the ship had covered a mighty 386 nautical miles. Reports were the weather was clear, fine and calm. Passengers were enjoying exploring the luxury liner and things were going well. More reports of ice had reached the Titanic by the 12th April. Ships who were sailing the route had confirmed the ice, although this was some distance from the ship at this point. As passengers later reported, the air temperature was cooling and the ship was making rapid progress, having covered 1065 nautical miles in two days.

Above; Luggage being carried aboard by ship's crew-members from a tender.

Main: The last photograph of Titanic. Father Browne's last picture of the White Star Liner RMS Titanic, leaving the port of Queenstown (Cobh) in Ireland at 1.55pm, Thursday 11th April 1912, on her maiden voyage to New York.

According to some passengers who survived, the cooler temperatures signalled ice being much closer to the ship, although it seemed that most passenger accounts and the reports from the crew demonstrate a lack of concern regarding the ice. Like the fire in the boiler room, it was not unusual for the ice to be around this part of the Atlantic and the reports from other ships that were to come did not bring cause for concern either.

On the westward leg of the Atlantic journey, Titanic was carrying only roughly half of her passenger capacity. This would later prove to be a blessing, as many more lives could have been lost during the impending disaster. Making it a few hours past *"the corner"* where the steamships would change course to head toward New York Harbour, the Titanic encountered the iceberg.

Above; Iceberg Warning Diagram.
Parallelogram of five ice warnings.

Main; Doug Spedden Playing on Deck.

*Main; Titanic silhouetted against
Cork Head on her maiden voyage.*

One passenger, a second-class British woman, Charlotte Collyer, survived her husband, who was also aboard the Titanic on its maiden voyage. Recalling her story in Semi-Monthly magazine in May of 1912, Collyer described the voyage:

"From our deck which was situated well forward, we saw the great send off that was given to the boat. I do not think that there had ever been so large a crowd in Southampton and I am not surprised that it should have come together. The Titanic was wonderful, far more splendid and huge than I had dreamed of. The other crafts in the harbour were like cockle shells beside her and they, mind you, were the boats of the American and other lines that a few years ago were thought enormous. I remember a friend said to me, 'Aren't you afraid to venture on the sea?', but now it was I who was confident. 'What, on this boat!', I answered. 'Even the worst storm could not harm her.' Before we left the harbour I saw the accident to the New York, the liner that was dragged from her moorings and swept against us in the Channel. It did not frighten anyone, as it only seemed to prove how powerful the Titanic was.

I don't remember very much about the first few days of the voyage. I was a bit seasick and kept to my cabin most of the time. But on Sunday 14th April I was up and about. At dinner time I was at my place in the saloon and enjoyed the meal, though I thought it too heavy and rich, No effort had been spared to give even the second cabin passengers on that Sunday the best dinner that money could buy. After I had eaten, I listened to the orchestra for a little while, then at nine o'clock or half past nine I went to my cabin. I had just climbed into my berth when a stewardess came in. She was a sweet woman who had been very kind to me. I take this opportunity to thank her for I shall never see he again. She went down with the Titanic.

'Do you know where we are?' she said pleasantly, 'We are in what is called the Devil's Hole.' 'What does that mean?' I asked. 'That is a dangerous part of the ocean,' she answered. 'Many accidents have happened near there. They say that icebergs drift down as far as this. It's getting to be very cold on deck so perhaps there is ice around us now.' She left the cabin and I soon dropped off to sleep. Her talk about icebergs had not frightened me, but it shows that the crew were awake to the danger. As far as I can tell we had not slackened our speed in the least."

Above; Titanic leaving Southampton with tugs assisting.

THE FATEFUL DAY

The Collision

Sunday 14th April 1912 was a tragic, fatal day. On calm waters, in cold and clear conditions, the Titanic sailed the usual course around to *"the corner"*.

The early morning of this fateful day was very bright and clear. The Titanic was not the only ship sailing the waters at the time. At 9am, the nearby RMS Caronia issued a warning of *"bergs, growlers and field ice"*, which was received and acknowledged by Captain Smith. The Titanic continued its journey.

Being a Sunday, Captain Smith then presided over a church service at 10.30am for first-class passengers. Held in the dining room, the service was the start to another fine day steaming along on flat, glassy water out at sea. Some accounts have attributed the conditions at the time to a mild winter, which caused icebergs to slip away from Greenland and move across the North Atlantic Ocean. High tides also meant there were more in this area, along the steamer route.

Other research conducted by various historians and academics has reviewed at length the weather conditions and the impact this would have had. Historian Tim Maltin concluded the calm sea would have created an optical illusion called Fata Morgana. According to the historian, the cold calm waters would have limited the ability to look out for icebergs and for nearby ships to see the Titanic. While not yet confirmed, this theory is one of many as to the reason or reasons contributing towards the Titanic's collision with the iceberg.

With flat conditions and a moonless, pitch-black night, it would have been difficult to spot icebergs close by. Winds generating whitewater and waves would have made for less pleasant conditions, but may have made easier spotting of icebergs for the lookouts. The lookouts had been given clear instructions to be on the watch for icebergs.

"I know this isn't scientific, but this ship's warning me she's gonna die and take a lot of people with her."

Thomas Andrews, Managing Director of Harland and Wolff

HOW A LINER WOULD LIGHT UP HER TRACK & AVOID DANGEROUS OBJECTS AHEAD

Above; How a liner would light up her track and avoid dangerous objects ahead.

Main; Work in progress on the 25-ton propeller shaft bracket of the new Cunard liner 'Caronia'.

Main; How lights fitted to a liner, by either oscillating or revolving, could create a pathway of light.

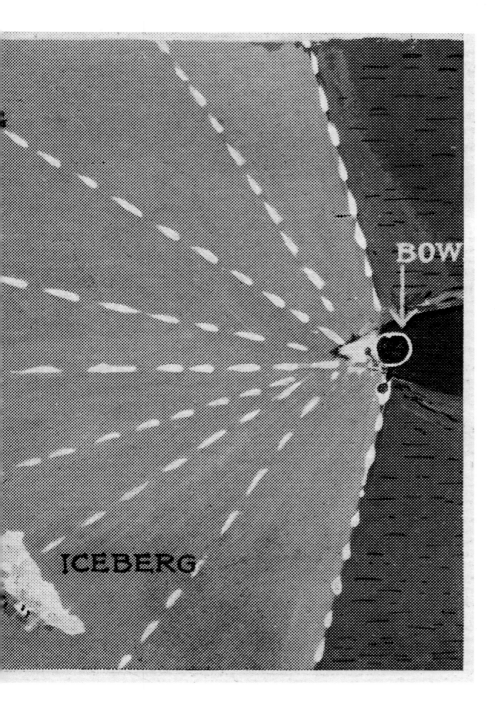

BOW

ICEBERG

In addition to the weather conditions, the lookouts had apparently complained of the lack of provision of binoculars. It was standard for lookouts to use binoculars and it seems unusual they were not provided for such an important, large and innovative ship's first voyage. Some accounts state there were binoculars aboard, but were locked away and without an available key to access them. Regardless of this claim, with the light conditions and circumstances surrounding the ship's collision, it has been deemed unlikely that binoculars would have given the lookouts the chance to spot the icebergs early enough to avoid real danger.

Above; Binoculars from the Titanic.

*Above; A pocket watch displaying the time
ten minutes to two, which was recovered from the
body of Titanic steward Sidney Sedunary.*

The Titanic received six warnings of ice
that day. However, it was considered
not unusual and Captain Smith's speedy
journey through the waters was not reckless. He had,
though, been steadily increasing the ship's speed
and was reportedly impressed with the new liner's
capabilities. Anticipating an early arrival in New
York, Smith did not appear to be concerned by
the warnings.

However, as evening fell, the air temperatures
dropped dramatically, with a recording of 33°F by the
time of 7.30pm. In freezing temperatures, the radio
operators received incoming reports of drifting
ice. Now dangerously close, the ice was reportedly
noticed by some passengers during the course of the
afternoon. While not all these messages were passed
on, reportedly because the operators were busy
sending messages on behalf of paying customers
aboard the ship, there was sufficient warning of
floating ice in the waters.

*Right; Illustration from French newspaper
Le Petit Journal, April 28, 1912.*

LA PERTE DU PLUS GRAND PAQUEBOT DU MONDE

Le "Titanic" a sombré après être entré en collision avec un iceberg

Concours du Supplément
du PETIT JOURNAL
N° 4

Main; The iceberg that sank the Titanic, view from
SS Carpathia which picked up survivors.

By early afternoon, the Titanic received more reports of ice. Another ship sailing the route, the RMS Baltic, had received warnings from Greek ship, Athenia, that they were *"passing icebergs and large quantities of field ice"*. Sending the message on to Titanic at 1.42pm, Smith also acknowledged the report. This time, he showed the report to Ismay and reportedly set a new course for the ship, to travel farther south.

Just three minutes later, another ship, the German liner SS Amerika, issued a report they were passing two large icebergs. Unfortunately, this message did not reach Smith or his officers, the reasons being unclear.

While the captain and crew and Ismay were aware of the danger of icebergs, apart from the reported change of course for the ship, the speed of the Titanic was not adjusted. Continuing to steam ahead at 22 knots, which is the equivalent of 41km per hour or 25 miles per hour, it was a mere 2 knots short of the liner's maximum speed. Considering the sheer size of the ship and the icy conditions, this was later deemed to be too high. However, for the captain and crew, it was not unusual to rely on lookouts for any dangers ahead and not to adjust speed for ice.

Believing in timekeeping and schedules, the White Star Line's captains and crews often went close to full speed. Even though the Titanic was built for comfort, luxury and grandeur and not for speed, the timely arrival of the vessel was still important.

In addition, in the early 1900s ice was not considered high risk on the open water, as there had not been any major incidents causing loss of life for liners of this size before. Smith's actions have been determined by some to be standard for the time and not unsafe. Captains and officers treated ice reports as warnings and not necessarily threats of real danger. Large liners had collided head on with icebergs previously and Smith had been famously quoted as saying before captaining the Titanic, that he could not "imagine any condition which would cause a ship to founder. Modern shipbuilding has gone beyond that." Indeed, other ships had survived collisions and limped home.

"We do not care anything for the heaviest storms in these big ships. It is fog that we fear. The big icebergs that drift into warmer water melt much more rapidly under water than on the surface and sometimes a sharp, low reef extending two or three hundred feet beneath the sea is formed. If a vessel should run on one of these reefs half her bottom might be torn away."

Captain Smith, Captain of Titanic

Main; John George 'Jack' Phillips. Wireless Operator on Titanic, he was serving as senior wireless operator on board Titanic. Titanic was sinking as Phillips worked tirelessly to send wireless messages to nearby ships for help, he did not survive.

Said to be engrossed in sending messages for passengers, the radio operator on shift in the evening of 14th April, Jack Phillips, had a backlog to issue via the station at Cape Race in Newfoundland. On receiving three more messages, Phillips apparently did not send them to the bridge.

At 7.30pm, the SS Californian messaged *"three large bergs"*. Later, at 9.40pm the steamship Mesaba sent a strong warning, *"Saw much heavy pack ice and great number large icebergs. Also field ice."* Unbelievably, Phillips cut off a third message, again from the Californian, this time at 10.30pm. Sending back the message, *"Shut up! Shut up! I'm working Cape Race."* Phillips could not have realized the significance of the repeated warnings of ice. The Californian had decided to stop its journey and stayed stationary for the night.

At 11.40pm, Frederick Fleet, the lookout on shift, alerted the bridge to an iceberg. Ringing the lookout bell three times, Fleet called the bridge and spoke urgently with Sixth Officer James Moody. Accounts state Moody asked, *"What do you see?"* to which he was answered, *"Iceberg, right ahead!"*

Main; Mr Murdoch was the officer in charge at the moment the Titanic encountered the ice floe and was on the Bridge at the moment of impact, He did not survive.

Moody immediately relayed the message to Murdoch, who was in charge while Smith was retired to bed. First Officer Murdoch immediately ordered the ship to be steered, *"Hard a'starboard"*, to attempt to avoid the iceberg. It was too late.

Unable to turn such an enormous ship fast, that was moving at considerable speed, Murdoch's attempt to avoid the iceberg by putting the engines in reverse and steering it were to no avail. Although managing to avoid a head-on collision, Murdoch could not avoid hitting the iceberg altogether. Ringing *"Full Astern"* on the ship's telegraphs, it was too little time to save the ship from collision.

It has been suggested that Murdoch's instruction was an attempt at a maritime manoeuvre called a *'port around'*, where an obstacle is avoided by steering the ship's bow around first, followed by the stern. Given the size of the liner, the speed at which the engines were powering it and the steam machinery, there would have been a delay and difficulty in setting the engine in reverse. Some analysis of this resulted in criticism of Murdoch's decision. While not proven, there were reports that attempts to stop the engine and put it in reverse hindered the ability to steer the ship. This same theory concludes that the Titanic may have avoided the iceberg if the ship had continued at speed and was steered around.

Main; Titanic survivor, ship's officer Lightoller, right, arrives at Liverpool on the 'Adriatic'.

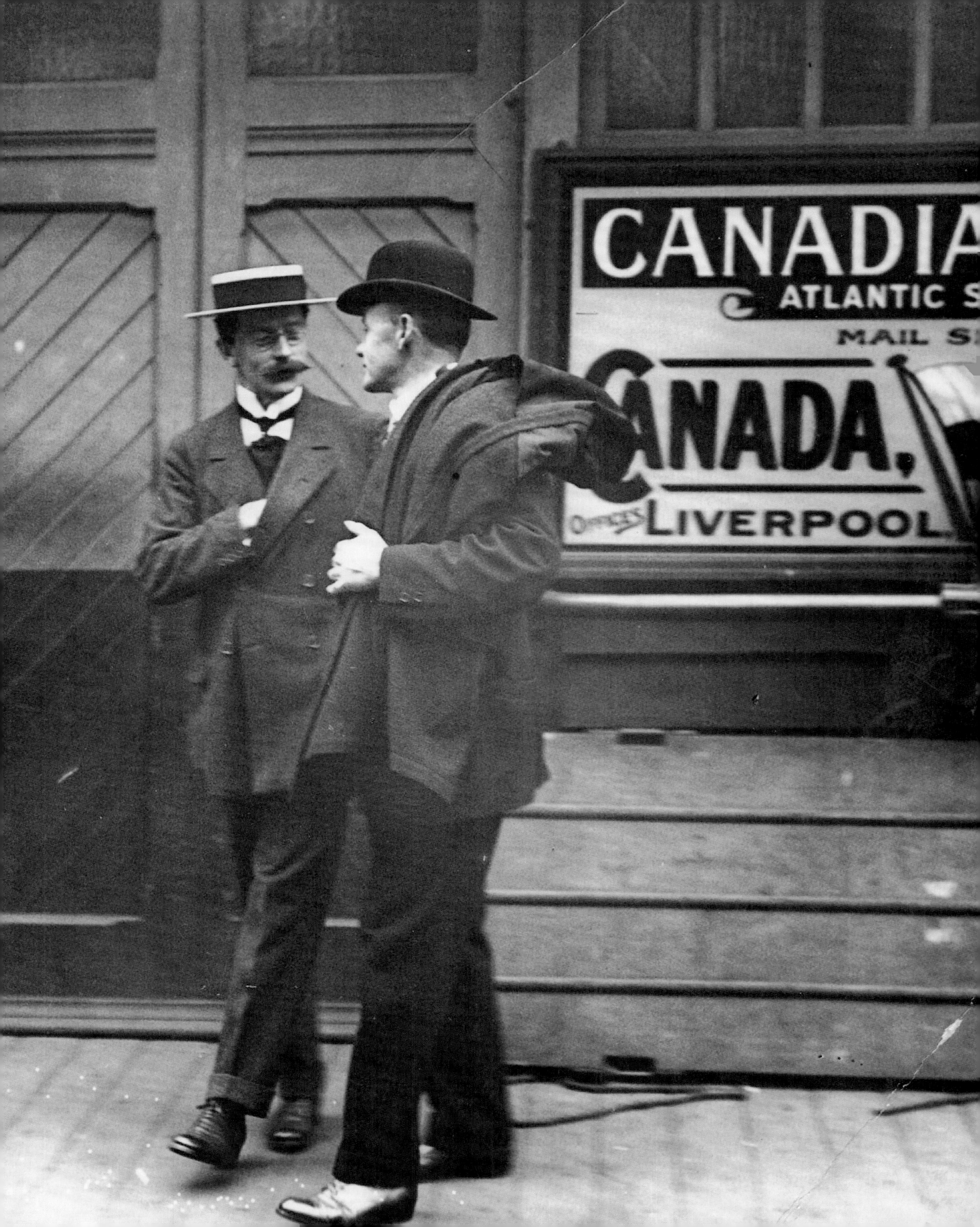
CANADIA
ATLANTIC S
MAIL S
CANADA,
OFFICES LIVERPOOL

Some have argued the Titanic's rudder was partially to blame for the collision. Despite the advancements in construction and design and technology, the rudder design was too small and not enough consideration was given to how the ship might turn in the event of an emergency.

"Just then the ship took a slight but definite plunge - probably a bulkhead went - and the sea came rolling along up in a wave, over the steel fronted bridge, along the deck below us, washing the people back in a dreadful huddled mass. Those that didn't disappear under the water right away, instinctively started to clamber up that part of the deck still out of water and work their way towards the stern, which was rising steadily out of the water as the bow went down. It was a sight that doesn't bear dwelling on – to stand there, above the wheelhouse and on our quarters, watching the frantic struggles to climb up the sloping deck, utterly unable to even hold out a helping hand."

Charles Lightoller, Second Officer

Above; Samples of steel from Titanic's hull.

Main; A half the size replica of the ill fated Titanic cruise liner is wowing crowds in rural Tennessee. Costing £16 million, the replica ship which is billed as the world's largest museum attraction is the second such ½ scale reproduction in the United States.

Striking the iceberg on the starboard side, the Titanic's hull had been torn open causing the levels below waterline to flood. It was reported the water quickly filled up to Deck F in the Mail Room. The preparations Harland and Wolff had put in place to create a buoyant ship in the event of an emergency had little effect when it came to the impact of the iceberg. Reports on the damage from the iceberg state that the steel plates had buckled under the pressure of the iceberg, causing the rivets to pop and open up a series of holes. Tearing a series of holes in the side of the ship, five of the watertight compartments had been compromised and were flooded. Only four of the 16 compartments could be flooded and secured from the rest of the ship to render it able to float.

Despite a head on collision being avoided, the iceberg caused irreparable damage. The iceberg was originally thought to have ripped open the hull in a large tear. Following the British Inquiry, the chief naval architect for Harland and Wolff, Edward Wilding, stated, *"I believe it must have been in places, not a continuous rip"*. This meant a series of openings, which resulted in flooding a number of compartments. After the wreck was discovered in 1985, subsequent surveys of the damage show there were six narrow openings along the length of hull, covering 1.1 to 1.2 square metres (12-13 square feet). Using ultrasound technology, the gaps were measured by Paul K. Matthias, who declared the damage consisted of a *"series of deformations in the starboard side that start and stop along the hull ... about 10 feet [3.0 m] above the bottom of the ship."*

The collision did generate a series of holes, the longest of which was 12 metres (39 feet) long, resulting in the rivets snapping and seams of the steel plates opening up. This allowed water to rush in and quickly fill the compartments in the hull.

Main; Passenger liner RMS Titanic, striking an iceberg on her maiden voyage from Southampton - Artist impression.

At the British Inquiry, the engineer testifying from Harland and Wolff actually suggested this but was apparently not believed. In fact, the pieces of the hull plates from the wreck show the steel shattered on impact. Whilst it was deemed at the time impossible for steel to break, it seems the iceberg had shattered pieces. This allowed the water to pour in at an estimated volume of approximately seven tons a second, making it impossible to stop or pump back out. Considering the fatal damage happening below the surface, ironically there was no visible evidence of damage above the waterline and many survivors, including crew, recalled on investigation that there did not appear to be anything wrong following the collision.

"Just before going to my state room, A11, there was a bump. As I turned the handle of my room [door] there was another bump. As I got into my room, there was a third bump. One of these bumps... like little pushes, nothing violent. I slipped on a coat over my white satin evening dress and went right out from my own state room because my state room had a door leading to the promenade deck. As I got out onto the promenade deck, I saw a large grey, what looked to me like a building, floating by. But that "building" kept bumping along the rail and as it bumped it sliced off bits of ice [which] fell all over the deck. We just picked up the ice and started playing snow balls. We thought it was fun. We asked the officers if there was any danger and they said, "Oh, no, nothing at all, nothing at all, nothing at all. Just a mere nothing. We just hit an iceberg."

First-class passenger Edith Louise Rosenbaum Russell

For many passengers who felt the movement generated by the collision, it seemed nothing was particularly wrong. Stewards working in first-class reported assuming the ship had lost a propeller. Obviously, those on the lower decks felt the collision a lot more greatly. Walter Hurst, who was on the crew as an Engine Oiler remembered being *"awakened by a grinding crash along the starboard side. No one was very much alarmed but knew we had struck something"*. In another crew survivor account, Fireman George Kemish heard a *"heavy thud and grinding tearing sound"*.

Captain Smith, who had earlier in the evening attended a dinner in his honour, had retired to bed after speaking with his First Officer Murdoch, where he had requested he be woken should anything concern the crew.

Smith reportedly rose on noticing the collision and went immediately from his cabin to the bridge to understand what had happened. On hearing of the iceberg, he summoned Thomas Andrews to help him inspect the damage. By the time they went below, the crewmen were battling to pump water back out of the Number 5 Boiler Room. With boilers full of hot steam, the pressure of the containers presented more risk to the ship if they were met with freezing cold water. Ordering the stokers and fireman to reduce the fires and release steam, the men worked hard while waist deep in seawater.

Main; Mr Thompson, a fireman on board , arrives at Liverpool on board the Adriatic.

THE BUCKLED PLATES

BILGE KEEL

FIRST CLASS STATE ROOMS

POST MAIL ROOM

DOUBLE BOTTOM

KEEL

ICE PENETRATING THE DOUBLE BOTTOM

The forward cargo holds, Mail Room and Number 6 Boiler Room were already flooded, as was the squash court. Observing the damage and knowing that the Titanic would only float if any four compartments (in certain combinations) were flooded, the ship was fast running out of time.

The engine rooms and boiler rooms had vertically closing doors that were controlled automatically and took a mere 30 seconds to close. However, the lower deck compartments were not sealed at the top. If too many compartments flooded and the boat was not even or level, the water would tip over into each causing more damage and flooding. With five compartments flooded, more than the number that would allow the ship to float, the ship would continue to flood and sink.

Now the Titanic was beginning to tip, having shifted starboard side. In just 45 minutes following the collision, water was flooding in around 15 times faster than the crew could pump it back out.

Andrews informed Smith the ship would sink in two hours.

Main; The Launch Of Olympic. Known As 'Old Reliable', She Was The Sister Ship Of Titanic And Britannic.

Main; 1997 Leonardo DiCaprio and Kate Winslet in James Cameron's Titanic.

AFTER THE COLLISION

The Sinking Ship

Just two hours and forty minutes after the Titanic collided with the iceberg in the Atlantic Ocean, the mighty *'unsinkable ship'* sank. Causing the deaths of 1,500 people, it became the biggest maritime disaster in history.

From the time the Titanic collided with the iceberg, it began sinking. With an estimated 35,000 tons of seawater inside the ship by the time she sank, at first the liner listed starboard. Then as water poured through passageways she reportedly listed portside and more flooding occurred. The Titanic began to sink bow-first, causing more water to spill over the compartments, creating a sharper angle as she went down.

Without a formal tannoy system or announcement system, passengers were still sleeping as the ship began to sink. Relying on stewards to wake unaware passengers, many did not have a chance to evacuate. In first-class, there were enough stewards to get to more cabins than in second and third-class, where stewards had many more passengers to manage.

Above; 'Wreck of the Titanic: appalling disaster '.
Headline from a newspaper.

"Deeply regret advise you TITANIC sank this morning after collision with iceberg, resulting in serious loss of life. Full particulars later."

J. Bruce Ismay, Director of the White Star Line

Again, without a system or protocol to follow, stewards and passengers were left to act as they saw fit in the circumstances. Because of their being convinced the ship could not sink, many passengers simply did not believe they were in trouble. When passengers were ordered to put on their lifejackets, at quarter past midnight, many were reported to have thought it was a joke.

Above; Life preserver from RMS Titanic.

Main; A never before seen in public life preserver from RMS Titanic on 18th June 2008 that will be sold during the Christie's New York annual Ocean Liner sale to take place on 25th June. The life preserver, one of only six in existence, has been kept in a safe by a Nova Scotia family since being found immediately after the 1912 disaster.

Being on the lower levels, third-class passengers seemed to matter less, with many trapped as the water filled up around them. Confronted with the sight of water flooding in, one of the few third-class survivors Carl Jansson remembered, *"Then I run down to my cabin to bring my other clothes, watch and bag but only had time to take the watch and coat when water with enormous force came into the cabin and I had to rush up to the deck again where I found my friends standing with lifebelts on and with terror painted on their faces. What should I do now, with no lifebelt and no shoes and no cap?"*

Main; Cross section of the Titanic to show how passengers got on to deck.

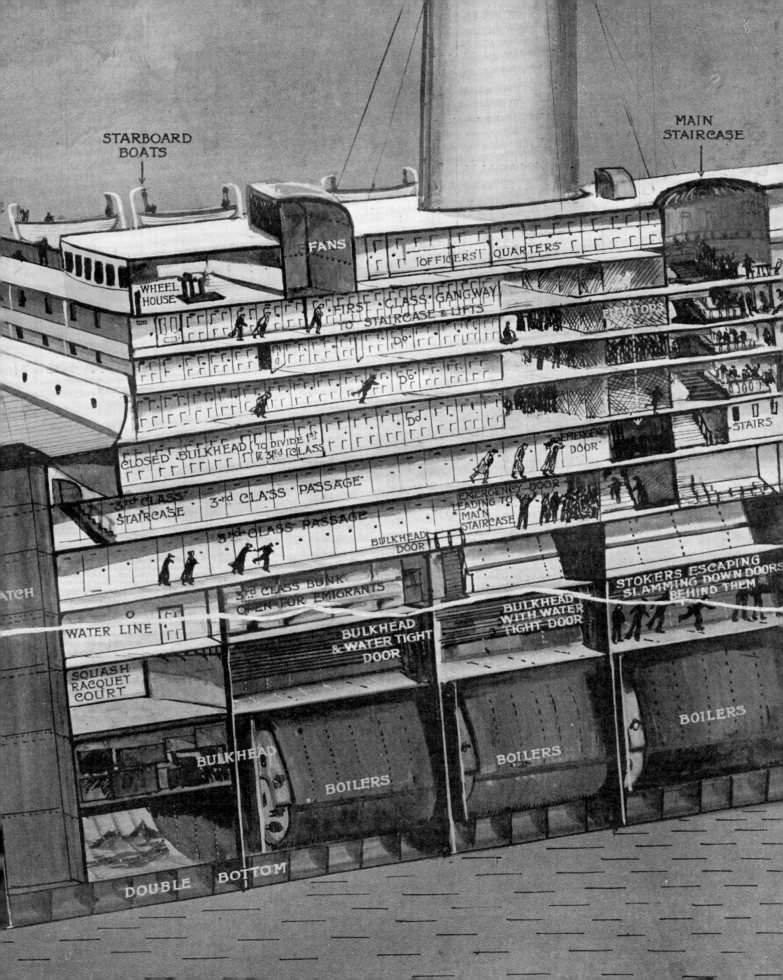

STARBOARD
BOATS

MAIN
STAIRCASE

WHEEL
HOUSE

FANS

OFFICERS' QUARTERS

FIRST CLASS GANGWAY
TO STAIRCASE & LIFTS

Do

Do

Dd

ELEVATORS

STAIRS

CLOSED BULKHEAD (TO DIVIDE 1st
& 3rd CLASS)

EMERGENCY
DOOR

3rd CLASS
STAIRCASE

3rd CLASS PASSAGE

3rd CLASS PASSAGE

EMERGENCY DOOR
LEADING TO
MAIN
STAIRCASE

BULKHEAD
DOOR

STOKERS ESCAPING
SLAMMING DOWN DOORS
BEHIND THEM

3rd CLASS BUNK
OPEN FOR EMIGRANTS

BULKHEAD
WITH WATER
TIGHT DOOR

ATCH

WATER LINE

BULKHEAD
& WATER TIGHT
DOOR

SQUASH
RACQUET
COURT

BOILERS

BULKHEAD

BOILERS

BOILERS

BOILERS

DOUBLE BOTTOM

Because the Captain had ordered the steam to be released from the boilers, the sound was so loud, survivor Lawrence Beesley described it as *"a harsh, deafening boom that made conversation difficult; if one imagines 20 locomotives blowing off steam in a low key it would give some idea of the unpleasant sound that met us as we climbed out on the top deck."*

At five minutes past midnight, Captain Smith ordered the lifeboats to be uncovered and women and children to be placed in the boats. Radio operators were instructed to send distress calls, which unfortunately were issued with the wrong coordinates. Rescuers were directed to the west side of the ice belt, about 13.5 nautical miles off from the Titanic's actual location.

In another unfortunate moment, the radio operator of the SS Californian, Cyril Evans, had decided to retire to bed just ten minutes before the Titanic collided with the iceberg. Then, a little over an hour later, the Californian's Second Officer, who was in command at the time, witnessed five white rockets exploding above the ship and called the Captain, Stanley Lord to ask what they meant.

Lord did not make any action or response to the report. Jack Phillips issued another distress signal over the Titanic's radio to the Russian ship SS Burma at 11.50pm.

Main; Rescuers from the ship Carpathia helping Titanic's radio operator Harold Bride off ship.

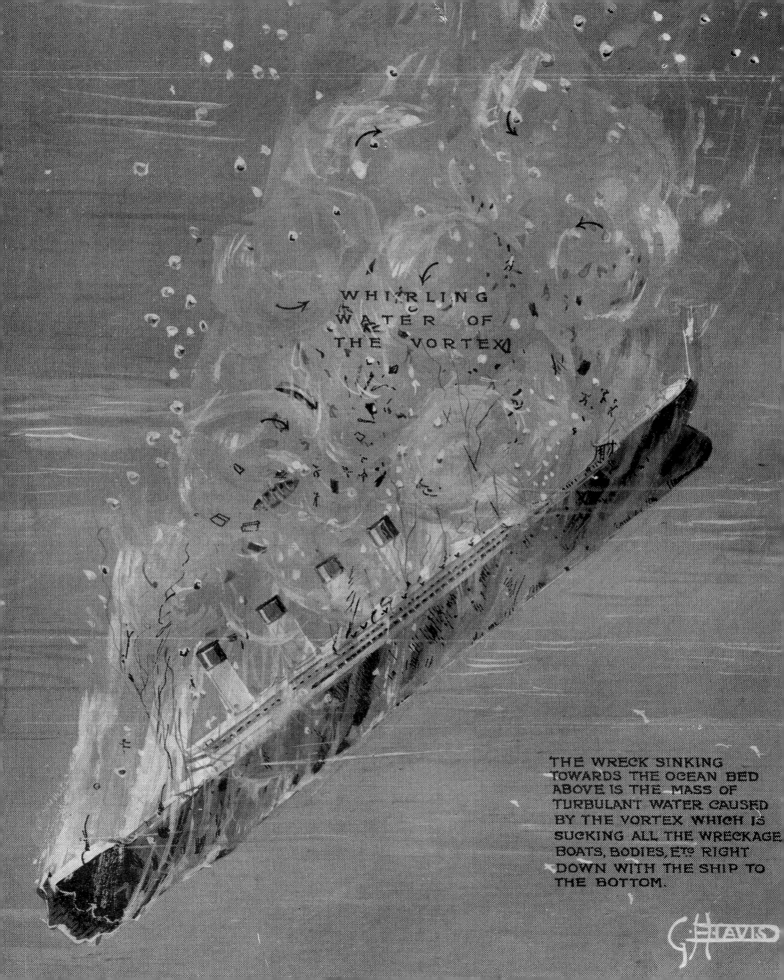

Despite accounts and stories told of the Titanic going down in one piece, the ship split apart between the third and fourth funnels as the stern tipped skyward. The immense pressure placed on the keel would have likely caused the split in two. The stern of the ship continued to rise skyward, almost at a 90 degree angle. Passengers were still clinging to the ship as it eventually sank.

By 2.15am, the gigantic liner's angle in the water intensified, with water pouring through deck hatches. Some survivors recalled the force of the angle tipped people into the sea and water rushing over the deck caused more to be swept away.

Interestingly, as a result of the American and British inquiries into the fatality, a number of surviving officers and survivors had testified the ship sank in one piece. Until the wreck was discovered, 73 years later, most people believed it went down whole.

Above; Flags at half mast, Queenstown (Cobh),
in mourning for the Titanic.

"The oarsman laid on their oars and all in the lifeboat were
motionless as we watch Her in absolute silence. Save some
who would not look and buried their heads on each
other's shoulders."

Lawrence Beesley, Titanic Survivor

Main; Illustration shows the wreck sinking towards the ocean bed, Above is the
mass of turbulent water caused by the vortex which is sucking all the wreckage,
boats and bodies down to the bottom with the ship.

Survivor Colonel Archibald Gracie said, *"Titanic's decks were intact at the time she sank and when I sank with her, there was over seven-sixteenths of the ship already under water and there was no indication then of any impending break of the deck or ship".*

"My friend Clinch Smith made the proposition that we should leave and go toward the stern. But there arose before us from the decks below a mass of humanity several lines deep converging on the Boat Deck facing us and completely blocking our passage to the stern. There were women in the crowd as well as men and these seemed to be steerage passengers who had just come up from the decks below. Even among these people there was no hysterical cry, no evidence of panic. Oh the agony of it."

Above; Titanic Distress Call. White Star Liner RMS Titanic's distress call (CQD and SOS) sent by Marconi Radio Officer Jack Philips by wireless telegraphy and received by steamship SS Burma at 11.50pm on Sunday 15th April.

Main; An artist's impression of the Titanic sinking. This illustration was originally published in The Sphere on 27th April 1912.

*Above; Chief Officer Henry F Wilde, First Officer
of the Titanic who went down with his ship.*

Some of the officers attempting to lower the two collapsible boats were caught up in this, with Murdoch and Wilde dying in the water. Officer Charles Lightoller made a remarkable escape and survived. He recalled abandoning his post and diving in the water, where he was nearly sucked into a ventilation shaft. By a stroke of luck, Lightoller was then blown clear by what he described "a terrific blast of hot air" and landed near a capsized lifeboat. On entering the water, he said *"Striking the water was like a thousand knives being driven into one's body. The temperature was 28 degrees, four degrees below freezing."*

Described by first-class passenger Jack Thayer, the pressure of the sinking caused huge shudders, *"Occasionally there had been a muffled thud or deadened explosion within the ship. Now, without warning she seemed to start forward, moving forward and into the water at an angle of about fifteen degrees. This movement with the water rushing up toward us was accompanied by a rumbling roar, mixed with more muffled explosions. It was like standing under a steel railway bridge while an express train passes overhead mingled with the noise of a pressed steel factory and wholesale breakage of china."*

*Main; Lowering the lifeboats on the SS Titanic
after the liner collided with an iceberg.
Original Publication: From a page of The Graphic, 1912.*

DRAWN BY CHARLES DIXON, R.I.

LEAVING THE SINKING LINER: A PERILOUS MOMENT FOR THE LIFEBOATS

"'Stop lowering 14,' our crew shouted, and the crew of No. 14, now only 20 feet above, cried out the same. The distance to the top, however, was some seventy feet, and the creaking of the pulleys must have deadened all sound to those above, for down she came—fifteen feet, ten feet, five feet—and a stoker and I reached up and touched the bottom of the swinging boat above our heads. The next drop would have brought her on our heads. Just before she dropped, another stoker sprang to the ropes with his knife open in his hand. 'One,' I heard him say, and then 'Two,' as the knife cut through the pulley-ropes. The next moment the exhaust stream carried us clear."—Mr. Beeston's narrative.

*Main; All that was left of the greatest ship in the world - the
lifeboats that carried most of the 705 survivors.*

For some on board, they must have believed there was no escape. They stayed in their cabins, waited down below and many others gathered together to pray. It was reported Father Thomas Byles, a priest and passenger on board, heard confessions and the band was said to have continued to play outside. Survivor Violet Jessop reported that she heard the hymn "Nearer, My God, to Thee" being played. This famous story attached to the sinking of the Titanic was never confirmed and conflicted with Archibald Gracie's personal account of the sinking. *"I assuredly should have noticed it and regarded it as a tactless warning of immediate death to us all and one likely to create panic."*

Rescue ship, SS Carpathia's bandmaster George Orrell said, *"The ship's band in any emergency is expected to play to calm the passengers. After Titanic struck the iceberg the band began to play bright music, dance music, comic songs – anything that would prevent the passengers from becoming panic-stricken … various awe-stricken passengers began to think of the death that faced them and asked the bandmaster to play hymns. The one which appealed to all was 'Nearer My God to Thee'."*

For those fortunate enough to escape safely and witness the ship's sinking, it was shocking and devastating. Lawrence Beesley described it, *"revolving apparently around a centre of gravity just astern of midships,"* and *"partly a groan, partly a rattle and partly a smash and it was not a sudden roar as an explosion would be: it went on successively for some seconds, possibly fifteen to twenty".*

Then the lights on the Titanic flickered and went out forever. Jack Thayer recalled *"groups of the fifteen hundred people still aboard, clinging in clusters or bunches, like swarming bees; only to fall in masses, pairs or singly as the great after part of the ship, two hundred fifty feet of it, rose into the sky."*

About this time people began jumping from the stern, my friend Milton Long and myself stood beside each other and jumped on the rail. We did not give each other any messages for back home cause neither thought we would ever get back."

The ship sank in only a few minutes, with more than one thousand passengers and crew members still on board. The now two separate parts of the ship were reported to have landed approximately 600 metres (2,000 feet) apart from each other on the bottom of the ocean. The momentum generated from the bow section sinking meant it settled into the ocean's bed 20 metres deep (66 foot). The stern part of the ship continued its descent on a vertical angle to bottom of the seabed, with external structures ripping off as it went down. From the wreck discovery, it was determined the decks had flattened on top of each other and more debris from the ship would have continued to descend for a number of hours after the body of the ship hit the floor.

Exposed to the freezing cold waters, most of those thrown into the ocean died by drowning, of heart attacks or of hypothermia from the -2°C waters. Of the hundreds of people in the water, lifeboats rescued a mere 13 more. Sadly, there was apparently room for nearly 500 more people who could have been saved.

"Many brave things were done that night but none more brave than by those few men playing minute after minute as the ship settled quietly lower and lower in the sea...the music they played serving alike as their own immortal requiem and their right to be recorded on the rolls of undying fame."

Lawrence Beesley, Titanic Survivor

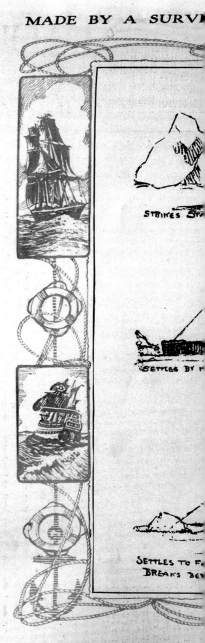

MADE BY A SURVI...

STRIKES S...

SETTLES BY...

SETTLES TO F...
BREAKS BE...

SHOWING THE LINER BREAKING
OF THE VESSEL'S COLLAPS...

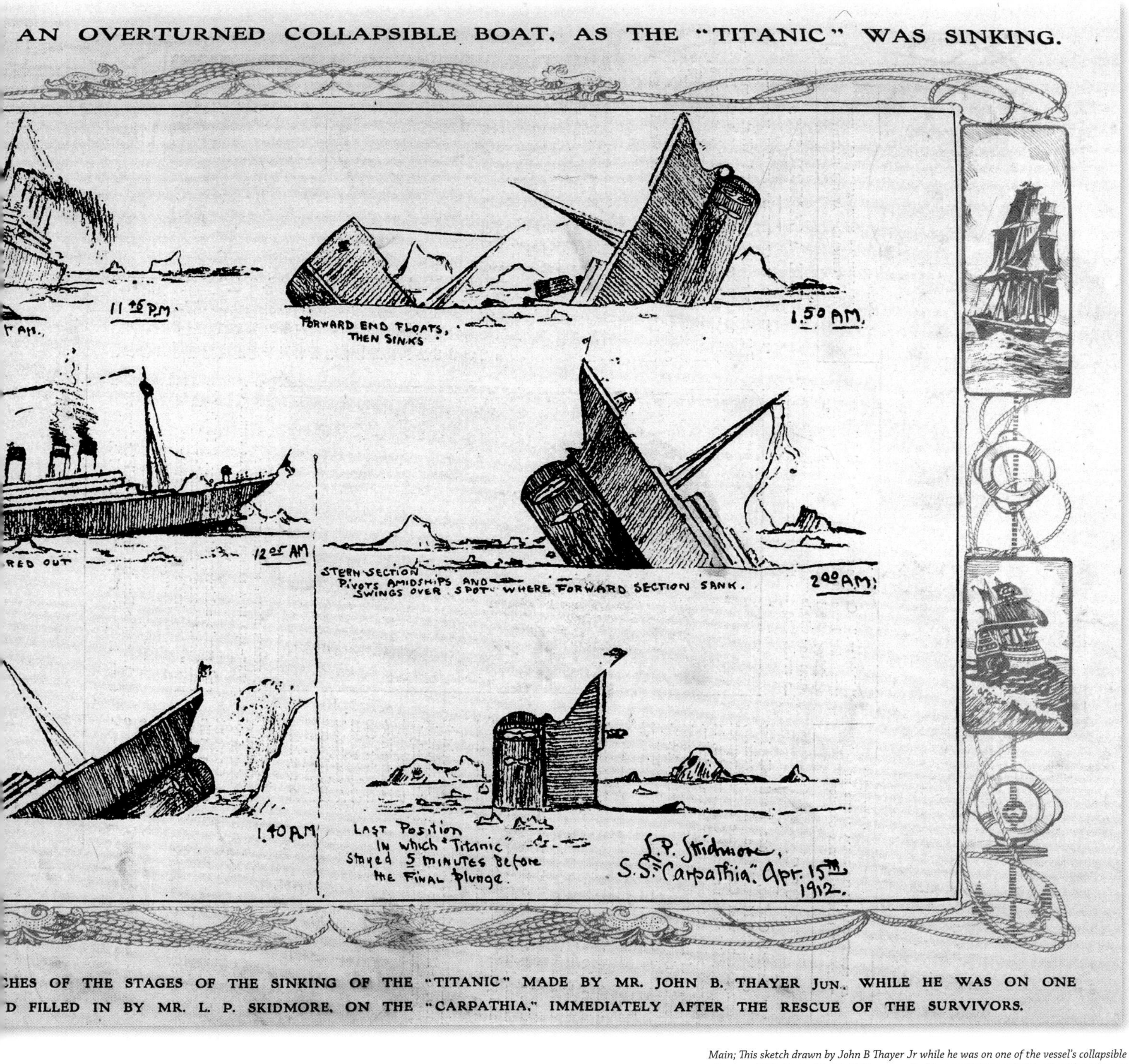

AN OVERTURNED COLLAPSIBLE BOAT, AS THE "TITANIC" WAS SINKING.

11⁵⁵ PM.

FORWARD END FLOATS,
THEN SINKS.

1.50 AM.

⁵ AM.

12⁰⁵ AM.

RED OUT

STERN SECTION
PIVOTS AMIDSHIPS AND
SWINGS OVER SPOT WHERE FORWARD SECTION SANK.

2⁰⁰ AM.

1.40 AM

LAST POSITION
IN WHICH "TITANIC"
STAYED 5 MINUTES BEFORE
THE FINAL PLUNGE.

L. P. Skidmore,
S. S. "Carpathia" Apr. 15ᵗʰ
1912.

...CHES OF THE STAGES OF THE SINKING OF THE "TITANIC" MADE BY MR. JOHN B. THAYER Jun. WHILE HE WAS ON ONE
...D FILLED IN BY MR. L. P. SKIDMORE, ON THE "CARPATHIA," IMMEDIATELY AFTER THE RESCUE OF THE SURVIVORS.

Main; This sketch drawn by John B Thayer Jr while he was on one of the vessel's collapsible boats and filled in by Mr P L Skidmore on the 'Carparthia' immediately after the rescue of the survivors' shows the liner breaking in two and the following disintegration.

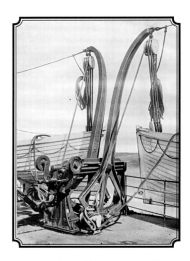

*Above; A pair of the Welin Davits on board Titanic
used to lower the lifeboats into the water.*

There was no doubt the ship, crew and passengers were unprepared for this moment. Having boarded the luxury liner with the assumption the ship could not sink, there was still apprehension from passengers about leaving the ship. The lifeboats had only capacity for half of the total number of people on the liner. If the Titanic had journeyed with its full capacity of just under 3,400 people, only a third of those would have been able to get a place on a lifeboat. While the steamship had more than met its maritime safety requirements for the number of lifeboats provided, clearly in the event of an emergency exit, it was nowhere near enough.

In addition to the shortage of lifeboats, apart from the Able Seamen, the crew were inadequately prepared and trained for such an emergency evacuation. It was reported that even the officers were not aware of how many people could be launched in the lifeboats and panicked launching them half full.

Of the process required for loading and lowering lifeboats, much criticism followed. In the dock, it was claimed only one lifeboat drill had been run and it was in itself inadequate, with just two boats lowered. Manned by one officer and four men each while rowed on the river, they were hardly tested for sea worthiness. In addition, the boats were meant to be stocked with emergency supplies, but were only partially so. It was also reported that lifeboat and fire drills had not been held while out at sea.

According to Lightoller, Smith ordered the *"women and children in and lower away"*. His account recalled Smith needed prompting, although it is unconfirmed exactly how it happened, *"I yelled at the top of my voice, 'Hadn't we better get the women and children into the boats, sir?' He heard me and nodded reply."*

It was recounted that this order was understood by Murdoch to be women and children first, although Lightoller believed it meant women and children only. In addition to the confusion, many passengers remained unconvinced that they should leave the large ship for small lifeboats. One story told how millionaire John Jacob Astor declared: *"We are safer here than in that little boat."*

Accounts of the lifeboat debacle included one story that as the pulleys used to lower the rope were freshly painted, they were stiff and kept getting stuck as they attempted to lower the lifeboats.

Main; A scene from the movie 'Titanic' which was nominated for a record-tying 14 Academy Awards.

aced with the reality that there were too few lifeboats to save everyone, the evacuation was futile for many. With more than 27 years captaincy experience, Smith must have been struck with fear at the reality and the horror of the situation. Having ordered the lifeboat release and loading of passengers, he had still not made an evacuation call, or organised and informed his crew of the severity of the situation. While he may have done so to prevent panic, it meant his officers were unprepared for the sequence of events to come. The lack of organisation meant that Fourth Officer Joseph Boxhall reported not being aware of the ship's sinking until almost an hour before the ship went down.

Some testimonials from the US Senate Inquiry that followed the epic disaster featured officer's accounts that they had believed the lifeboats might break if they were lowered while full.

Margaret Brown described the scene in an interview with The New York Times: *"The whole thing was so formal that it was difficult for anyone to realise it was a tragedy. Men and women stood in little groups and talked. Some laughed as the boats went over the side. All the time the band was playing ... I can see the men up on deck tucking in the women and smiling. It was a strange night. It all seemed like a play, like a dream that was being executed for entertainment. It did not seem real. Men would say 'After you' as they made some woman comfortable and stepped back."*

Main; Captain Edward Smith, giving his last orders to the crew of the doomed White Star liner.

In the instance of one lifeboat that was launched, the plug was missing or had come out somehow which meant the lifeboat was flooding. It was secured with *"volunteer contributions from the lingerie of the women and the garments of men,"* said survivor Dorothy Gibson.

There are countless other stories about the lifeboat crisis as the Titanic sank, many of which are unconfirmed and unsubstantiated. They include stories about passengers still on board the ship attempting to sneak on the lifeboats, one being threatened at gunpoint to get back and allow women and children on first and another of a male passenger who allegedly boarded a lifeboat by covering himself in a woman's shawl.

Main; English actor Kenneth More (1914–1982) as Second Officer Charles Herbert Lightoller fires his pistol into the air in a scene from Roy Ward Baker's 1958 film 'A Night To Remember'.

Main; The ship gradually sinking from 1997 film 'Titanic.'

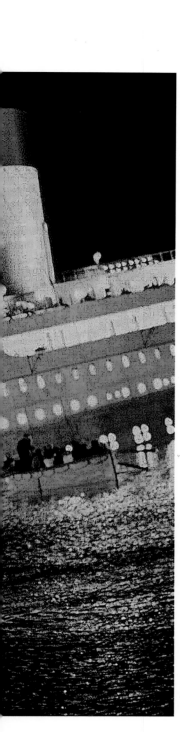

Of those who managed to secure a place on a lifeboat, the majority were first and second-class passengers. Because of strict US immigration laws at the time, immigrants had to be sectioned away from the rest of the population in case of diseases. In fact, it was standard practice that third-class passengers participated in health checks on arrival at New York.

Nonetheless, following the tragedy and the evacuation chaos of the Titanic, the crew was criticized for preventing the third-class passengers from escaping.

The month after the sinking, Irish survivor Margaret Murphy wrote:

"Before all the steerage passengers had even a chance of their lives, the Titanic's sailors fastened the doors and companionways leading up from the third-class section … A crowd of men was trying to get up to a higher deck and were fighting the sailors; all striking and scuffling and swearing. Women and some children were there praying and crying. Then the sailors fastened down the hatchways leading to the third-class section. They said they wanted to keep the air down there so the vessel could stay up longer. It meant all hope was gone for those still down there."

Survivors who were safely in lifeboats had to then get through the freezing conditions at night. And, worse, the people in the lifeboats suffered the sounds of the poor souls who were dying in the sub-zero waters.

Lawrence Beesley said of the experience, *"every possible emotion of human fear, despair, agony, fierce resentment and blind anger mingled – I am certain of those – with notes of infinite surprise, as though each one were saying, 'How is it possible that this awful thing is happening to me? That I should be caught in this death trap?'"*

The shock must have been horrendous. Beesley continued that the experience *"came as a thunderbolt, unexpected, inconceivable, incredible. No one in any of the boats standing off a few hundred yards away can have escaped the paralysing shock of knowing that so short a distance away a tragedy, unbelievable in its magnitude, was being enacted, which we, helpless, could in no way avert or diminish."*

The other survivors would be haunted by the screams and moans. George Rheims, one of the few who survived the icy waters, said it was *"a dismal moaning sound which I won't ever forget; it came from those poor people who were floating around, calling for help. It was horrifying, mysterious, supernatural."*

"The sounds of people drowning are something that I can not describe to you and neither can anyone else. It's the most dreadful sound and there is a terrible silence that follows it," said Eva Hart.

Above; A replica Titanic lifeboat is pictured at the Titanic Belfast visitor centre in Belfast, Northern Ireland.

Many of the survivors had naively assumed everyone had been rescued and on hearing the crying, the pain and agony of death, were mortified. Lady Duff-Gordon, remembered *"the very last cry was that of a man who had been calling loudly: 'My God! My God!' He cried monotonously, in a dull, hopeless way. For an entire hour there had been an awful chorus of shrieks, gradually dying into a hopeless moan, until this last cry that I speak of. Then all was silent."*

Fifth Officer Lowe said there were *"hundreds of bodies and lifebelts"* and that the dead *"seemed as if they had perished with the cold as their limbs were all cramped up."*

The sounds ceased after 20 minutes and Lowe recalled that he *"waited until the yells and shrieks had subsided for the people to thin out"* and then gathered five of the lifeboats together to transfer passengers to make room for more in one of the lifeboats. Heading back to the site of the sinking, he took a crew of seven and a volunteer to try to save more. His account recalled that most of those in the water had died by this point.

Waiting to be rescued, the survivors rowed to keep warm and attempted to keep spirits up. It was cold, bitter and there were not any provisions or lights for comfort.

Above; How the News of the Sinking of the Titanic Reached Londoners.

Main; sailors in rescue boat shining torch on passengers from sunken Titanic in cold sea.

*Main; Life boat drill, Holland America Line -
putting boats over the side.*

As the next day dawned, the survivors were exhausted. Having had to dispose of the bodies of those who did not survive the night, the remainder was weary and feeling low. Archibald Gracie, who was sat on top of a collapsible boat that was upturned, wrote of *"the utter helplessness of our position."* As the wind picked up it became more difficult to keep it balanced.

With so few survivors, from a ship that was touted by many to be unsinkable, the news caused a public outrage.

Relaxed maritime regulations, the lack of lifeboats, treatment of third-class passengers and the resulting fatalities led to the introduction of the International Convention for the Safety of Life at Sea (SOLAS) in 1914. SOLAS continues to govern shipping and maritime safety today.

Above; How the News of the sinking of the Titanic reached Londoners.

THROUGH THE ICY WATERS

Waiting for Rescue

A number of ships had received the distress signals of the Titanic. Three ships raced to get to the Titanic's location. A risk to all the crews on board these vessels, they too had to navigate through the icy waters that the Titanic had encountered its demise in. The Carpathia was the closest ship and would reach the scene first.

One and a half hours after the Titanic sank, the RMS Carpathia arrived to rescue the survivors aboard lifeboats. By 9.15am the morning of 15th April, the rescue was complete. Shockingly, less than a third of those aboard the Titanic survived. Sadly, some survivors died during the rescue from injuries and exposure, some dying on board the rescue ship. Those who did make it through were now being safely brought on board the Carpathia.

Above; The Carpathia arrives to pick up survivors in lifeboats.

"There was peace and the world had an even tenor to its way. Nothing was revealed in the morning the trend of which was not known the night before. It seems to me that the disaster about to occur was the event that not only made the world rub its eyes and awake but woke it with a start keeping it moving at a rapidly accelerating pace ever since with less and less peace, satisfaction and happiness. To my mind the world of today awoke 15th April 1912."

Jack Thayer, Titanic Survivor

Main; Titanic Lifeboats. Photograph taken from the RMS Carpathia.

*Main; Captain Sir Arthur Henry
Rostron KBE RD RNR 1869 to
1940 Captain of RMS Carpathia
of the Cunard Line when it rescued
survivors from RMS Titanic.*

The Carpathia had travelled through the night at high speed to reach the scene of the sinking. The ship's captain, Arthur Rostron, had ordered his crew to keep the boilers at full pressure, to generate the most speed possible. It was the first rescue call Captain Rostron had taken in his career. He knew what to do and firmly ordered his crew to ready this ship with ladders, blankets, hot drinks and medical aid. Rostron had also rigged lights on the side of the ship and readied gangways to make the rescue more efficient.

Above; British mariner Sir Arthur Henry Rostron

"We set foot on deck with very thankful hearts, grateful beyond the possibility of adequate expression to feel solid ship beneath us once more."

Lawrence Beesley, Titanic survivor

*Main; How the Titanic
survivors were picked up by
the Carpathia.*

Some survivors reported seeing the lights of the rescue ship around 3.30am, which must have been a huge relief. Of the historians who state that Jack Phillips' radio message contained the wrong coordinates, it was reported the Carpathia had reached the location only to find there was nothing there. According to one report, the crew from the Carpathia saw a light, possibly a flare, from one of the lifeboats and found the survivors and the scene of what was left of the Titanic.

Above; Where she lies in the Atlantic, diagrammatic illustration showing the location of the wrecked Titanic in the Atlantic ocean.

Lifeboat 2 was the first to have its passengers brought aboard, at 4:10 am. The first passenger to be lifted to the rescue ship was reportedly Elizabeth Walton Allen, a first-class passenger. Lifeboat 12 was the last. Thirteen lifeboats were brought on board and were later taken to the White Star Line's Pier 59 in New York. Nothing remains of the lifeboats today. After workmen (who wanted to keep a piece of history) removed Titanic nameplates and their equipment, the company did not store the lifeboats. It is unknown where the lifeboats ended up. Some have assumed there were destroyed, while others surmised they were used on other White Star Line ships.

*Main; Survivors of the Titanic disaster boarding a tug from the
liner which rescued them. of main shot.*

Because the rescue took hours, sadly another survivor died just before they were able to board Carpathia. Helped by the crew of the rescue ship, survivors were either brought up in slings or mail sacks, or if they were able to pulled them up. On board, some family members were reunited. Others would have their hopes dashed. The scenes on board the rescue ship were described as both joyous and sad. Some were in shock at their loss and at their experiences.

"At 8:30 all the people were on board. I wanted to hold a service, a short prayer of thankfulness for those rescued and a short burial service for those who were lost. While they were holding the service I manoeuvred around the scene of the wreckage. We saw nothing but one body."

**Captain Arthur H. Rostron,
Commander of Carpathia**

The scenery out to sea was a shock to the crew of the Carpathia. As daylight came, there were what looked to be huge ice fields, with the Captain, Arthur Rostron claiming to have seen 20 large icebergs, which he estimated measured up to 61 metres high (200 feet). Upon surveying this scene, the crew must have realized the risks they themselves had taken to race to rescue the survivors of the Titanic.

Captain Rostron then ordered their route be set for New York, where the survivors could be attended to and left the other two rescue ships who had by now arrived on the scene. After another two hours of searching by the crews on the ships, there were no more survivors to be found.

Above; Captain Arthur Henry Rostron, R,N,R,, aged 43, was commander of the Carpathia.

*Main; how Titanic encountered the iceberg
stream from Greenland.*

Main; Crowds waiting for arrival of survivors of the disaster.

arpathia and her heroic crew arrived three days later in New York, the evening of the 18th April. Having journeyed through difficult weather and allegedly ice, fog, thunderstorms and rough seas, the survivors must have been overjoyed at arriving back on dry land. Around 40,000 people were there at the waterfront to greet the rescue crew and survivors. Arriving at Pier 34 in New York, the Titanic survivors disembarked. The news of the ship's disaster had not reached the wider public at this point and there was a public outcry at the news of such loss.

Above; Survivors of the Titanic disaster, picked up by the Carpathia arriving in New York.

Rostron and his crew were honoured for their actions in saving the lives of those evacuated from the Titanic. Survivor Margaret Brown presented the captain with a silver cup and the crew each received a medal in the ceremony. Cunard Line, who owned the Carpathia, also reportedly awarded their employees with a month's wages in recognition for their valiant efforts. Rostron was also decorated with the distinguished Knight Commander of The Order of the British Empire, or KBE, a rarely issued and highly recognized honour.

Upon hearing of the huge loss of life, the White Star Line chartered a number of ships to recover the bodies of the dead. Undertakers and members of the clergy joined the crew for the recovery. Because health regulations required only embalmed bodies could be accepted, the ships carried embalming supplies. According to some reports, 333 bodies were found and brought back to be buried.

Above; Captain Arthur Rostron and under officers of RMS Carpathia (Cunard), with loving cup presented to him by survivors of wreck of RMS Titanic.

CUN
Royal & Unit

NOTICE.

The Steamers of this Line now come alongside the Liverpool Landing Stage, and London Passengers depart from or arrive at the Riverside Station on the Quay adjoining.

Paddle Wheel R.M.S. "Britannia," 1840. Length 207 feet. 1,139 tons.

CAMPANIA   12,950 tons.   Captain H

RD LINE

States Mail Steamers.

THIRD-DAY PASSAGES.

ESTABLISHED 1840.

ANTIC FLEET.
R.N.R.

Twin Screw R.M.S. "Campania" and "Lucania," 1893.
Length 620 feet. 12,950 tons.

Main; An advertisement for the Cunard liner
R.M.S. Campania.

Above; Outside the White Star offices at Southampton showing people searching for the names of loved ones amongst the list of survivors

CS Mackay-Bennett, one of the Canadian cable ships charted for the grim job, found so many bodies that they soon ran out of embalming supplies. The first ship to reach the site of the sinking, the cable ship CS Mackay-Bennett found so many bodies that the embalming supplies aboard were quickly exhausted. The captain of the ship then ordered only the bodies of first-class passengers should be embalmed. The decision to do so was based on the reasoning that they would need to identify the bodies of those with large estates and wealth to be distributed and would prevent any disputes over wills. Because the health authorities would not accept any bodies that were not embalmed, many of the crew of the Titanic and third-class passengers were buried at sea.

There were many complaints that followed the captain's decision, from families and from undertakers. Of the bodies preserved, they were shipped to the closest city with rail and steamship connections, in Halifax, Nova Scotia. To cope with the number of bodies, the city set up a temporary morgue in a curling rink. Family members then travelled to identify the bodies of their dead and were shipped to their hometowns for burials. However, there were still 150 who were not identified, the majority of whom were buried in local cemeteries.

Main; Relatives of Titanic disaster victims, 1912.

Main; The Titanic Memorial at Belfast.

Later, in May of 1912, the RMS Oceanic found three more bodies over 320 kilometres (200 miles) from where the Titanic sank. After this, the bodies of the remainder of victims were never recovered.

Memorials were established in New York, Washington, Southampton, Liverpool, Belfast and Lichfield and ceremonies were held in the US and the UK to commemorate the dead and raise funds to aid the survivors. In Southampton, women gathered at the White Star Line's offices, crying, wanting to know if their loved ones were alive. The people of Belfast were devastated. Shipbuilders were said to have openly cried in the streets on hearing the news. Many in Ireland have said a sense of shame, guilt and grief hung over the city following the tragedy. Belfast's churches were overrun with people grieving, praying and trying to make sense of the disaster. It was said that, for a long time, Belfast carried great sadness from the Titanic's end. And the shipbuilders and workers who helped create it felt guilty and responsible.

Public inquiries followed, with the first in the United States, chaired by Senator William Alden Smith. It was very soon after the event, beginning on the 19th April. The 18 days of investigation involved questioning survivors and rescuers, with over 80 witnesses called on. The first to be questioned was Ismay, then officers and crew followed. The inquiry also called on expert witnesses to help establish the conclusions.

Presented on the 28th May to the US Senate, the final report included some of the following excerpts:

- *The Captain had shown "indifference to danger [that] was one of the direct and contributing causes of this unnecessary tragedy."*

- *The SS Californian had been "much nearer [to Titanic] than the captain is willing to admit"*

- *"No general alarm was given, no ship's officers formally assembled, no orderly routine was attempted or organised system of safety begun."*

- *The British Board of Trade bore responsibility "to whose laxity of regulation and hasty inspection the world is largely indebted for this awful tragedy."*

Senator Smith's final report included much more detailed findings and then concluded, *"The calamity through which we have just passed has left traces of sorrow everywhere; hearts have been broken and deep anguish unexpressed; art will typify with master hand its lavish contribution to the sea; soldiers of state and masters of trade will receive the homage which is their honest due; hills will be cleft in search of marble white enough to symbolize these heroic deeds and where kinship is the only tie that binds the lowly to the humble home bereft of son or mother or father, little groups of kinsfolk will recount, around the kitchen fire, the traits of human sympathy in those who went down with the ship. These are choice pictures in the treasure house of the affections, but even these will sometime fade; the sea is the place permanently to honour our dead; this should be the occasion for a new birth of vigilance and future generations must accord to this event a crowning motive for better things."*

He then proposed legislation that included a re-evaluation of the maritime legislation and a commission to enquire into laws and regulations regarding the construction and equipment of ocean vessels. New acts were introduced that required better management of radio (including continuous monitoring) and wireless onboard vessels.

Though the British government and media were displeased with the accusatory tone of the US investigation, the British inquiry, conducted by Lord Mersey on 2nd May, came to relatively similar conclusions with a few exceptions. Most notably, the British Board of Trade was not overly criticized as it was in the US.

Main; American politician Senator William A. Smith (1859-1932) of Michigan walks to the US Senate inquiry into the RMS Titanic sinking, 1912. The hearings took place in New York and Washington between 19th April and 25th May.

Above; Lord Mersey, One of the two presidents of the official inquiries in to the sinking of the Titanic.

Taking testimony from close to 100 witnesses, over a 36-day investigation, it became the longest, most detailed of any court of inquiry in Britain. Interest from the media and public piqued when Captain Lord's officers, who had appeared intimated by their commander, contradicted Lord.

In addition, the inquiry attracted a lot of attention when the Duff-Gordons, who had been accused of misconduct, stood for testimony. They were cleared of any wrongdoing.

Of the conclusions reached by the British Inquiry, the following were some of the findings:

- *The Californian "could have pushed through the ice to the open water without any serious risk and so have come to the assistance of the Titanic. Had she done so she might have saved many if not all of the lives that were lost."*

- *"The Court, having carefully inquired into the circumstances of the above mentioned shipping casualty, finds, for the reasons appearing in the annex hereto, that the loss of the said ship was due to collision with an iceberg, brought about by the excessive speed at which the ship was being navigated."*

- *The Captain had done "only that which other skilled men would have done in the same position." However, they determined that practice was not to be repeated, "it is to be hoped that the last has been heard of this practice. What was a mistake in the case of the Titanic would without doubt be negligence in any similar case in the future."*

The report's recommendations, along with those of the earlier United States Senate inquiry that had taken place in the month after the sinking, led to changes in safety practices following the disaster.

From the inquiries and evidence of the fateful maiden voyage of the Titanic, new safety measures were introduced, to ensure the key learnings were put to good use. It became compulsory to provide more lifeboats, carry out lifeboat drills and staff radio equipment on a full-time basis. In addition to the SOLAS regulations, an International Ice Patrol was also set up to monitor the North Atlantic.

*Main; Stewards who survived the Titanic shipwreck line up outside a first class
waiting room before being called in for questioning by the board of enquiry.*

In addition to the critical eye of the inquiries, the media and general public were critical of various leaders involved with the Titanic. Some of the criticism and scrutiny levelled at the men who held responsibility for the lives of so many was later deemed fair and some quite unfair.

Ismay had a more favourable public opinion in Britain than he did in the US. He was accused of being selfish and unheroic by boarding a lifeboat and yet at the British inquiry, Lord Mersey said, *'Had he not jumped in he would simply have added one more life, namely his own, to the number of those lost'.*

Ismay was also accused of ordering Captain Smith to beat the previous record for crossing the Atlantic, although this was never substantiated and was viewed by many as extremely unfair. Even today, his image is tarnished.

Interestingly, the individuals involved in the construction, journey and rescue were more heavily criticised than the organisations that governed them. While the public inquiries blatantly highlighted the need for change in maritime regulations, the media and public speculation appears to have focused more on the individuals involved.

What was to be a glorious journey of new technology and innovation in shipping and new horizons for many of the passengers on board, became a clear reminder of the power of nature over science and mankind.

Main; The Lord Mayor of London arriving at St Paul's Cathedral, London, for the memorial service for the victims of the Titanic disaster.

Picture Credits

Individual credits as follows:

6 Hulton Archive; 7 Bob Thomas/Popperfoto; 8 Popperfoto; 9 Universal Images Group; 10 Universal Images Group; 11 Topical Press Agency; 12 (t) Science & Society Picture Library, (b) Universal Images Group; 13 (t) Universal Images Group, (bl) Topical Press Agency, (br) Science & Society Picture Library; 14 Popperfoto; 15 FM Browne SJ; 16 Universal Images Group; 17 Topical Press Agency; 18 Universal Images Group; 19 Universal Images Group; 20 (t) Popperfoto, (b) FM Browne SJ; 21 (t) Universal Images Group, (b) Universal Images Group; 22 (t) FM Browne SJ, (b) FM Browne SJ; 23 Universal Images Group; 24 Popperfoto; 25 Science & Society Picture Library; 27 Topical Press Agency; 28 (t) Time Life Pictures, (b) Universal Images Group; 29 (t) Universal Images Group, (b) New York Daily News Archive; 30 FM Browne SJ; 31 Universal Images Group; 32 Bob Thomas/Popperfoto; 33 Topical Press Agency; 34 Science & Society Picture Library; 35 Science & Society Picture Library; 36 (t) Popperfoto, (b) Peter Muhly; 37 Hulton Archive; 38 (t) Science & Society Picture Library, (b) Peter Macdiarmid; 39 (l) Universal Images Group, (r) Roger Viollet; 40 Universal Images Group; 41 Hulton Archive; 42 Apic; 43 Topical Press Agency; 44 FM Browne SJ; 46 Matt Campbell; 47 Universal Images Group; 48 Topical Press Agency; 49 (t) Topical Press Agency, (b) Universal Images Group; 50 Universal Images Group; 51 (t) Don Emmert, (b) Universal Images Group; 52 Science & Society Picture Library; 53 Popperfoto; 54 (tl) Universal Images Group, (tr) Popperfoto, (b) Science & Society Picture Library; 55 (t) Universal Images Group, (b) Matt Cardy; 56 Universal Images Group; 57 FM Browne SJ; 58 Helen H. Richardson; 59 The Washington Post; 60 (b) Michelle Bennett; 61 FM Browne SJ; 63 Topical Press Agency; 64 Universal Images Group; 65 Topical Press Agency; 66 (t) Popperfoto, (b) Peter Macdiarmid; 67 (t) Bob Thomas/Popperfoto, (b) Universal Images Group; 68 Hulton Archive; 69 Time Life Pictures; 70 Matt Cardy; 71 Universal Images Group; 72 (t) Davison & Associates Ltd, (b) AFP Photo/Don Emmert; 73 (l) The Boston Globe, (r) Time Life Pictures; 74 Time Life Pictures; 75 Peter Muhly; 76 Topical Press Agency; 77 FM Browne SJ; 78 Science & Society Picture Library; 79 Hulton Archive; 80 (t) FM Browne SJ, 80 (b) Universal Images Group; 81 (l) Peter Muhly, (t) FM Browne SJ, (b) FM Browne SJ; 82 Time Life Pictures; 83 Universal Images Group; 84 Topical Press Agency; 85 Universal Images Group; 87 Universal Images Group; 88 Science & Society Picture Library; 89 Stock Montage; 90 FM Browne SJ; 91 Universal Images Group; 92 FM Browne SJ; 93 Topical Press Agency; 94 FM Browne SJ; 95 FM Browne SJ; 96 Universal Images Group; 97 FM Browne SJ; 98 Popperfoto; 99 FM Browne SJ; 100 Universal Images Group; 101 Keystone; 102 Universal Images Group; 103 Michel Boutefeu; 104 Matt Cardy; 105 Leemage; 106 Universal Images Group; 109 Universal Images Group; 110 Universal Images Group; 113 Topical Press Agency; 114 Barcroft Media; 115 John B. Carnett; 117 AFP; 119 Topical Press Agency/Stringer; 120 Hulton Archive; 122 Paramount Pictures; 123 British Library/Robana; 124 Timothy A. Clary; 125 Leon Neal; 127 Universal Images Group; 129 Time Life Pictures; 130 Universal Images Group; 131 Davison & Associates Ltd; 132 Universal Images Group; 133 Popperfoto; 134 Topical Press Agency; 135 Hulton Archive; 136 Universal Images Group; 139 Science & Society Picture Library; 140 Universal Images Group; 144 Merie Wallace; 142 Hulton Archive; 145 John Pratt; 146 Paramount Pictures; 147 Peter Muhly; 148 Universal Images Group; 150 Buyenlarge; 151 Universal Images Group; 152 Hulton Archive; 153 Universal Images Group; 154 Universal Images Group; 155 Hulton Archive; 156 Universal Images Group; 157 Universal Images Group; 159 Hulton Archive; 160 Universal Images Group; 161 Universal Images Group; 162 Universal Images Group; 163 Hulton Archive; 164 Universal Images Group; 165 Hulton Archive; 166 Universal Images Group; 167 FPG; 168 Fox Photos; 171 Stock Montage; 172 Universal Images Group; 173 Topical Press Agency; 174 Topical Press Agency.